To Eva.
with hopes that sometime
she will take a look at
the Russian land

The

RUSSIAN

Land

with respect

Albert Rhys Williams

25 / I / 28

The Russian LAND

by ALBERT RHYS WILLIAMS

NEW YORK
NEW REPUBLIC, INC.
1927

For permission to reprint parts of THE RUSSIAN LAND thanks are due the *Atlantic Monthly, Asia,* and the *New Republic.*

The decorations have been taken from Russian school- and children's books

CONTENTS

I

IN THE DEAF VILLAGES OF THE NORTH

I

IN THE DEAF VILLAGES OF THE NORTH

"IF you want to know the peasant," said Kalinin, Russia's president, to me, "start in with one of our far away governments, go to some backward *volost*, and to the 'deafest' village. They'll be primitive, but informing."

In pursuit of the "deaf" villages—far away places into which the voice of the world does not penetrate—we found ourselves, after six days by river, at Pinega, two hundred and fifty miles in the wilderness east of Archangel.

[1]

Pinega is so remote that it was for centuries a place to which the tsar exiled his rebels; and here, to-day, we met a few banished enemies of the Soviet. It is so northern that it is drenched in summer with the perpetual light of the white nights; at first alluring to us, then nerve-irritating. It is so isolated that the first boat, coming after the ice-break-up in the spring, is hailed as a messenger out of another world.

For all this, Pinega didn't seem very primitive or deaf. And though the boat ran no further up the river, the road did. From this road for ten versts we could look back upon the glowing domed church that the Great Catherine had built as a spiritual outpost of her Empire.

Then, heading into the forest, our wagon joggled on for hours through pines and firs and larches. A sharp turn and out of this green-walled tunnel we emerged upon the river bank. Here before us, like a shimmering canvas, lay the flower fields of the Pinega, in this place eight miles long.

[2]

These meadows, that a few weeks earlier lay under the brown spring floods, were now flooded deep with flowers. It was as if the North, casting off her long winter's austerity, had flung herself into a madcap riot of flaming yellows and pinks and purples; as if all her colors and all her perfumes, finding no other vent, had here burst forth in a wild extravaganza. Through golden pools of buttercups and cascades of daisies, we plunged into blue seas of bluebells and red seas of clover. Above all, the giant Queen Anne's Lace raced and tossed like whitecaps before the stiff breeze blowing.

It was a magic breeze, for when it ceased the flowers vanished and only dark wheeling mosquito clouds danced before our eyes. Up from the earth, from all sides, they rose in blinding swarms. In size and vigor they were as remarkable as the flowers; the meadows had brought them forth together. Now, as if avenging the flowers crushed beneath our wheels, they fell upon us in battalions, stab-

[3]

bing our skins with their sharp lances, drawing blood in forty places.

"Devoured by mosquitoes," is here not just a phrase. In his "Year in the North," Michaelov describes two twelve-year-old berry-pickers driven into the bog by mosquitoes and perishing under their assaults. On the other hand, our driver was not even greatly annoyed by these stinging hordes. But that proves nothing. Like all Russian peasants, half hardened, half immune to pests, he would be equally indifferent in a room full of cockroaches or a bed full of a more bloodthirsty tribe.

Forewarned, we had armed ourselves with turpentine and citronella, usually discouraging to the ordinary mosquitoes; but these mosquitoes lapped them up like alluring nectars. We were sorry now that we hadn't brought along a highly recommended secretion of reindeer horn, one whiff of which would dismay a bear or a polecat.

The best device proved to be a special net (*komarnik*), which slipped down over our heads and hung to our waists in long folds like a veil, transferring us into a sort of etherialized Ku Klux Klansmen. Even so arrayed, an occasional lusty mosquito came plunging through the meshes. This was irritating, still one could bear it.

Quite unendurable, however, was the humming that went on ceaselessly, maddeningly, within half an inch of our ears, without let-up, without change of key. The right vibrating note of a violin, long maintained, it is said, will set the steel framework of a bridge or sky-scraper to rocking. That may not be true. But it is true that the ceaseless singing of mosquitoes will set the net-work of nerves a-jangling almost to the breaking point. Certainly these mosquito armies must have played their part in breaking the morale of the Allied Expedition which in 1918 floundered about in these forest bogs and fields.

"At midnight the cold comes and the mosquitoes go," said our driver reassuringly.

But he was wrong, for though it became almost freezing, this only served to tune up the mosquito choirs to a more exasperating pitch. They were water-proof too, quite heedless of the rain that now came drizzling down.

To pass from misery to misery, we began bumping over a long corduroy road running through a swamp. Under the horses' hoofs the logs moved up and down like piano-keys. Now sinking into the mire, now suddenly rising up, now holding firm, they sent a series of violent jolts through the wagon into our spinal columns.

From all this we were reduced to a half dazed condition. Through the weird spectral light that the white night poured over the landscape, we moved forward hour after hour, as in a dream. I remember now only indistinctly crossing a primitive rope-ferry, the rafters of a burned village rearing up like black skeletons, and our entry into the village of Pochezrye in sheets of rain.

Here I recall a big peasant generously welcoming us into his *izba*, driving out a couple of dogs, prodding up sleeping figures from the floor, saying, "Katya! Katya!" and lifting a little girl, scratching her face, out of a feather bed and motioning me into it. I literally fell asleep. Into its warm quiet depth I sank away from the pursuing light and rain and cold and mosquitoes, down into a featherly nirvana.

Ten hours later I was awakened by the entrance of the little girl Katya who was still scratching her face. I felt apologetic for having ousted her from her bed.

"What's the matter?" I asked.

"Smallpox! Black smallpox!" she feebly drawled.

"She's got chickenpox, or she's crazy!" I commented to myself, lapsing into sleep again.

This time I was aroused by her brother, hunting a birchbark pail. He was grumbling about having to go berry-picking alone.

"Why doesn't your sister go with you?" I asked.

"Sick," he replied, "she's got black smallpox."

"Smallpox!" I gasped.

"Yeh!" he answered nonchalantly. "That's why she slept in your bed instead of on the floor."

My hair rose on end, and I rose with them. No one ever got up out of a feather bed into his clothes and out of a room as fast as I did. I was off in a furious, frightened search of facts. I found them, each one more sinister than the other. Here they were without one redeeming feature.

Smallpox was epidemic in the village; fifteen had already died of it; the little girl Katya was just beginning to convalesce, and was, consequently, in the most infectious stage; there was no doctor in this village, nor the next, nor for fifty versts.

"A primitive, far-away 'deaf' village," Kalinin had recommended. Well, here it was, up to all specifications. And very informing too, quite as he had said. But was I going to bring this information out?

Being outraged at my big smiling host was

only fatuity. In sheer good faith and hospitality he had given me the best bed in the house.
What then was I so terribly wrought up over?
This he couldn't understand, nor could any of
the villagers who flocked around. They were
deeply interested in me as a man from America,
but not at all as a man who had just slept in a
smallpox bed. Most of them had been doing
that every night for a week or two. Then why
hadn't they gotten it? The germ theory I
talked about sounded far fetched and fanciful.
Better their own theory: To each man his des-
tined lot, and no escaping it; it's Fate that metes
out good and evil, life, death and smallpox.

"It's quite simple," said an old *mujik*, "you
get it or you don't. You die or you don't."
Incontrovertible, but distressing doctrine.

Amidst hearty "good-bys" and "come
agains," and with the pocked face of little
Katya peering at us from the window, we fled
the village. We made record speed, heedless
of mosquitoes, mud and jounces, our minds all
centered on calling up the symptoms of small-

pox and feeling them one by one creeping upon us. So we came galloping into Troophino, the *volost* center. Here was authority, and before it I laid my case solemnly, like an international incident. These peasant officials tried hard to be serious over it as I appeared to expect. But it was evident that the germ theory had feeble hold on them. Nor could they comprehend a person getting so excited over what might occur to him.

"But you got a good night's sleep," queried one old fatalist.

"Yes."

"And you haven't got smallpox?"

"No."

"Well, then, what are you worrying about?"

However, we did get here some encouraging information: There was a Medical Point at Peremen, thirty-six versts up the river. Vaccine had already arrived there, and the fight against infection was being carried on by the *feldsher* (assistant doctor) Popov.

"Devil take him!" laughed an old *mujik*,

limping about, slapping his sides. "He scratches skin off folks. If they swell up, he says they won't get smallpox. *Gospody! Gospody!* Lord! Lord!"

Scratching people with a needle to ward off disease: to such lunacy had they come in these degenerate days. His mirth-provoking ridicule would have been a delight to any anti-vaccinist. He himself was a champion of the remedies inherited from the fathers, the old charms and conjurations that have stood the test of time. These are by no means public property, but are still surrounded with secrecy. The incantation regarded as most efficacious against smallpox was to be three times repeated thus:

Saint Pantelimon! Saint Martyr Oor! Put out the fire; quench the pain; ward off the arrows of hell from thy servant . . . name.

Gnomes of the Forest! Send this bird of hell to the wild beasts; let it pock them with its beak.

Wicked Seed! Plant your roots into the earth, not into the face.

[11]

Clear Water! Pour thy cleansing floods upon the pocked face, and wash it smooth and clean.

All Saints! Pray for your suffering servant.

Whispered thrice, then written on paper, this spell was to be kept tied around the neck of the patient until he got well. If he didn't get well, if he died, it didn't imply that the incantation was at fault, it only implied that something was wrong in its recital.

This is not, as it might appear, simply a crafty evasion. For an incantation is based upon faith in the magic power of the Word. The exact words were fixed upon in a secret treaty, long ago, made with the unseen powers. To change one word, one syllable in the formula, is to break the spell. But to repeat these words rightly is to speed them from the tongue, like an arrow to its goal, and bring recovery to the patient.

This particular smallpox incantation is no longer all pagan; it has been modified by Christianity. The saints have crept in alongside the heathen gnomes. It has become half a prayer: a request to the unseen powers. The pure incantation is a command: a calling up of the secret treaty with full confidence in its automatic execution. Its usual ending is: "My word is sure" or "My words are firm, harder than stone, stickier than glue, saltier than salt, tougher than steel. What is meant, that shall be fulfilled."

So ends the incantation which Ivan Bogovoy, president of the Archangel Soviet, gave me as the accepted remedy for malaria: "Instead of our quinine," he said, "the sufferer is sprinkled with bog water, and with a spell they seek to drive out the devil spirits which they think are shaking him and rattling teeth."

In peasant theory evil spirits are at the root of most diseases. It has happened that the medical corps sent to relieve an epidemic have been taken as the evil spirits themselves. The peasants sought to get rid of the disease by killing the doctors. When the doctors arrived in the cholera districts of Kem, all doors were

[13]

barred and the women screamed at them from the windows:

"Go away, you devils! Why do you come here to kill our children?"

"Listen!" cried the doctors, "we come to save your children. To vaccinate them. You don't understand!"

"Yes, we understand very well!" cried the women, "you want to stamp them with the seal of Anti-Christ!"

All such preventive measures the peasants have looked upon as waste of energy. Like our old fatalist of Troophino, they believe that there is enough real trouble without worrying about something that doesn't yet exist. In rare cases, however, they sought to prevent the entry of plague by building a ring of bonfires around their village, and even scaring it off by gunfire.

The old beliefs, carrying down the centuries, though often deep concealed, still come flaming forth in crises. But they are dying. Faith in the old incantations is passing with the passing generation. Only the Old Believers kept up a stubborn fight against vaccination. The twelve million peasants that Russia sent to forty fronts in the great wars brought back to the village the ferment of new ideas—the new viewpoint. Now as we rode forward we were joined everywhere by people on horse and foot, pushing on to Permen, to the vaccination center.

Passing under a sign, "Sanitary Point," we enter a big rough-log room, filled with a long line of peasants, sleeves rolled up. It slowly moves forward towards a little white-aproned figure in a corner by the window. This the *feldsher*, Popov, pressing his silver lancet upon the bare arms, one by one, as they are brought before him. With a few quick strokes he scuffs off the skin, three crimson spots appear, and the next arm is laid before him. Scarcely looking up, he cries out occasionally:

"Keep line! Don't touch your arm!"

The circle moves slowly round again, and he rubs in the vaccine. Intent, concentrated, only the strange apparition of an American causes him to break his almost rhythmic motion.

[15]

I overwhelm him with questions about incubation period, fever symptoms, etc.

For answer he digs up a circular that came with the vaccine from the Health Commissariat. He reads it aloud, but in it there is nothing about these matters. He hasn't any books on smallpox. And if he did have books, how would he find time to read them? He has to tend all the sprains, fractures, cancers, hysteria, fevers, births and deaths, in a province as large as some whole kingdoms. On top of all this routine comes this scourge—he and his needle, alone, pitted against it.

Finishing off his ninetieth case for the day, we walk over to his house for dinner. There is much fish, for there has been a big catch on the river. So it goes: meat in plenty when the hunters have a run of luck; bread in plenty, if an August frost does not blight the crops. When all these fail, he falls back on the $3.00 a month he gets from the government—sometimes. He was stinted in income and training and equipment, but withal he was efficient.

[16]

The vaccination he gave me took beautifully.

It would never occur to him that he was brave. These men of the North are all brave. With them it is ever a hazard of life in cold and storm, flood and pestilence. Always living close to death; but always so calm and quiet and unexcited about it. It was quite strange to me.

And in their minds, this American, so unquiet, so very much agitated in the face of disease and death. That probably was a bit strange to them.

The farther we went up the river, the deeper we pushed into the Russian past. The streets with their big block houses were like Old Novgorod. A mist lifting from a village might be the curtain going up on a setting of "Prince Igor" in the Moscow Opera.

But these were real log houses, real peasant women in high fantastic head-dress, and peasant girls dancing in their rainbow colored costumes. Here were living conjurers and exorcisms to fire the hearts of fickle lads with love.

Here too were the *bilini*, the great epics reciting the valorous deeds of the mythical knights of old, taking us back into the very twilight of Slavonic history.

Once these *bilini* singers were found all over the vast reaches of Russia; now only in these forest fastnesses. And even here we hunted long. At last in Vigara, in response to our inquiries, the children said: "There she is our singing little grandmother—*babooshka!*"

And out of the little door of a little log house came a little old lady, more than eighty years of age and less than eighty pounds in weight. It was as if she came out of a fairy tale. But she had no magic powers and was heartbroken, because her table was bare—not even bread to offer us.

"It is only song we came for," we explained.

"Good!" she exclaimed. "I'll sing for you two weeks long." And forthwith she began the epic of Ilya, the Great Warrior of Prince Vladimir, the Russian King Arthur.

[18]

Ilya is the son of a peasant, for thirty-three years a cripple. Passing strangers give him a draught of water. Strength at once comes into his limbs. He feels that he can lift the earth. With his father's blessing, he fares forth against the bandits. The vibration of his bowstring hurls them from their horses. His arrow splits an oak to pieces. A stone, striking his head, rebounds and kills its thrower. He ties Nightingale Robber to his saddle and brings him a captive to Prince Vladimir, holding high revel in the halls of Kiev: Now begin his exploits against the Tartars.

"Aren't you tired?" I asked after listening half an hour to Ilya's defying the Tartar Khan.

She did not hear me. She was no longer in this little hut, but in distant Kiev, hearing the bells ring from the towers; riding with Ilya across the plains to battle. She was lost in her work, a perfect artist with perfect breath control. Her voice, although faint with its eighty years, was steadfast. It threatened to

[19]

flow on for hours. But at last Ilya killed the
Tartar Khan, and taking advantage of this, I
asked her to write some verses in my book. She
smiled and shook her head. She was illiterate.
Of all the *bilini* singers, hardly any can read
or write. They don't care to. "It puts out the
memory," they say.

Their memories are indeed astounding. Our
singer Marya Krivopolenova (Crooked-log)
knows one hundred thousand verses. More
than even has been written down by Ozorov-
skaya. Another, Fernov, knew seventy epics,
enough for two months' non-stop singing—
about ten thousand printed pages. But only
recently has this vast collection of poetry been
printed. It has been carried down the centuries
by word of mouth. Thus, the songs listened
to this day, passing on from generation to
generation, came at last to an old seal-fisher
of the Arctic. He was the uncle of our singer,
Marya. As a little girl she learned them, and
kept singing them through the gay days of her

life; through the gray years of hunger and wandering.

But there is no one to learn the old epics from her. She is the last of her race. The troubadours of France and the bards of ancient Wales have gone. Now, before one's eyes, in the North, one can see the great race of *bilini* singers passing away.

Why should boys and girls of to-day tax their memories with these epics when they soon may find them all in the books? How, too, can the old tales hold their thrill and glamor for a generation that has lived through ten years of war and revolution? To these peasants who marched away with twelve million fellow-peasants in the army of the Tsar, the armies of the past are rather insignificant. Insignificant, too, the travels of Ilya to the hunter of this village, who, with the Russian Division in France, marched under the Arch of Triumph and across the desert sands of Algiers. And to the lad, down river, who dropped a bomb on

[21]

a munition train and blew a whole town to bits, Ilya's smashing an oak to splinters doesn't seem so wondrous.

Moreover, how can any wonder of the far-away and long ago compete with an actual living wonder? And one has come right here in Chakolo village, two versts away. The children were impatient for us to see it. So bidding good-by to the last of the *bilini* singers, we hurried over to gaze upon this new wonder— the first, the only creamery for hundreds of versts along the Pinega.

We arrived in time to join the crowd marveling at the mystery of the strange machine separating cream from milk. It was a magic apparatus, doing in an instant that which for the peasant had always taken a day. The separator was from America, the churn from Germany and the molder from England. Thus Russian cream, completing its circuit, came forth delicious yellow butter.

To one who has known for months only the

poor, tasteless or rancid stuff that among the villagers passes for butter, it was a revelation. And when one saw out of the same sort of milk that the peasants spoiled issuing these appetizing golden creations, it was like a miracle.

The miracle-maker was a spare, slightly bent man with deep-socketed eyes, ascetic, intellectual—Peter Tabirin. Centuries ago he might have been Peter the Hermit, crusading against the Mohammedans. But living in this political age, he was Peter the Rebel, crusading against the Tsar, against the great war, against the Bolsheviks, against the Whites and, finally, crusading against all enemies of the Soviet. His life has been one of battle, hunger, arrest, prison, escape.

Weary of political strife, he flung it aside, and for two years gave himself to the study and practice of dairying. Now, with zeal backed by technical skill, he had become a fervent apostle of butter to these peasants of the Upper Pinega. He had chosen this village, Chakolo, for its hardy breed of cattle, able to graze a living out of the forest. Here, too, in the big bends of the river, were grass meadows and wide sweeping flower-fields. For crusaders, of course, there are only battle fields.

The life of strife left behind in politics, Peter Tabirin now took up on the economic front. He had to build a structure out of logs; to bring the machinery here and set it up; to train a staff of boys; to organize a Coöperative; to drill a peasantry in sanitation; to introduce the new concepts of science into minds casting off the old superstitions. To do all this one must have not only zeal and knowledge, but an understanding of the customs and prejudices of a backwoods Russian village.

Here, for example, when an animal is lost in the forest, the peasants consult the local wizard where to find it. Here, when a cow is up for sale, one may still hear an old *baba* saying: "No, she's the wrong color. The master will not like her!" The "master" whose taste in color is so respected is not, as one may suppose, her husband, but the house-spirit—the *domovoy*. He may like white cattle; on the other hand, he may prefer black or spotted. At all costs, he must be pleased; for it he dislikes the cow he may cause her to go dry or sick or lead her astray in the woods.

Not so long ago, scarcely any event was initiated without referring to the *domovoy*. Moving into the new house with a pot of burning embers, raked from the old stove, the peasant cried out, "Welcome, Grandfather, into the new house!" Bringing a newly purchased animal into the shed, the owner, bowing to each of the four corners of the building, said, "Here is a shaggy beast for thee, Master. Love him. Give him to eat and drink!"

But the days of the *domovoy* are nearly over. Talking with Igor, the fourteen year old chief of the churning squad, I said:

"Perhaps some of them will take up lodging in the new creamery."

"They have already!" he replied. "You can find them over there in the milk pails. Peter Tabirin calls them bacteria."

"So the old *domovoys* are all gone," I sighed with mock solemnity.

"Yes," he answered with a laugh, "they were all killed off in the Revolution."

Not only to the boys and soldiers, but even to many of the older generation the *domovoys* are dead. Other institutions and ideas, cherished for centuries, are likewise dying. They were picturesque to read about, but they held the village in darkness and fear, chaining it to the past. The Revolution came like a whirlwind blasting these old views, blowing away the miasmas and superstitions—breathing into the villages the impulse to a new life.

That's why Peter Tabirin, who once fought the Communist Revolution, now supports it. Devastating and destructive though it is, it clears the way for the future. It continues to release the forces that make possible enterprises like his. It lightens tenfold the tasks of the teacher and agronomist. Once these pioneers were voices crying in the village wildernesses. Sometimes they were driven out and even killed. Now the wilderness rises up eager to hear them and give heed.

One may still find in Russia thousands of villages sunk in muck and misery, festered with disease and ignorance—but no longer can one find villages that are deaf. Out of the slumber of ages they are waking to the new voices calling to them.

II
VLAS, THE OLD BELIEVER

II

VLAS, THE OLD BELIEVER

In the famine year, Kvalinsk bazaar was a place of the dead. The black log elevators stood empty-bellied as the people, the last grain blown from their cracks. No cattle, no dogs, nor cats, nor pigeons—all had been eaten. In the Bread Row the corpses were corded like wood.

That was five years ago. To-day the bazaar is stacked with food. Yellow piles of millet, green pyramids of watermelons, golden mounds

[31]

of wheat and rye. Most gay the red and rose mountains of the Apple Row, and moving amongst them a huge mountain of flesh on two short, stocky legs of enormous girth.

"How are you, Vlas Alexsevich?" I called to him.

"I'm two hundred and eighty pounds—five pounds gain this week," he replied exultingly. *"Slava Bogoo!* Glory to God. I'm recovering."

By "recovery," the old man meant getting back the three hundred and sixty pounds that hung upon his five-foot frame in the days before the Revolution. Then he was a veritable behemoth. But his was not the fat of sloth and indulgence, for, from the days when he went barefoot in winter, Vlas never spared himself.

A big wheat harvest across the Volga? There was Vlas buying early, rushing it across the steppe and up river to Kazan. Horses to buy from the Kirghiz a thousand versts away? There was Vlas, waging war on the natives who stole the laggard ones from his drove, stealing twice as many in revenge. A caterpillar raid on his orchards? No sleep nor rest for Vlas until the last pest was gone. A big wall-on-wall fight on *Maslanitsa?* Vlas was in the thick of it, his great ham fists swinging till the last man was down. Vlas carries the scars of battle. "My left ear knocked deaf by a whaling blow on my right ear," as he proudly explains.

No, Vlas' immense diameter was not the fat of inaction. He got it by taking to the table the same enterprise he took into work and business and fighting. In normal times this zest for food is quite abnormal, but on Saints' Days, surrounded by his many ikons and his dowager daughters, swathed in his Old Believer *kaftan*, waited on by his wife Shura— it passes all degrees of abnormality.

"Come on Saint John's Eve," urged the old man, "and bring your *baba.*"

We came at six to find Shura, majestic in a green *sarafan* with silver buttons reaching to

[33]

her feet, bringing on the *pirogi*, a kind of pasty.
A peculiar Slav failing are the *pirogi*. No
Russian housewife can rest easy with a plain
piece of dough. She is impelled to wrap it
round something—rice, liver, cheese, cabbage,
fish . . . anything she can lay hands on—
this, baked, becomes a *pirog*. There were five
kinds around the samovar and over all the
fragrance of cherry-tea.

"Fill the glasses to the brim!" said Vlas.

"The intelligentsia don't do that any more,"
corrected Shura, passing the tiny morsels of
sugar through which the Russians usually suck
their tea.

"The intelligentsia don't do that any more,"
snorted Vlas gleefully. "They put the sugar,
not in their mouths, but in their glasses." He
ran our glasses over with three splashing lumps,
and piled our plates with herring, sterlet, caviar
red and black, and eggs. Then sweets to satia-
tion, brined apples, pickled preserves, all-flower
honey and four sorts of spicy jams.

This, I presumed, was the supper. It proved

to be but a preliminary skirmish to a long series of soups, tongues, hams, fish, joints. Crowning all the great pies—ten American pies in one—almost rivaling Vlas in circumference, and following one another down into his enormous maw.

Vlas ate like an Old Believer of the old school. What that means one may find by turning to Gogol's story of Aphanasy Ivanovich. His stomach was in lineal descent from that old gormand, who after gorging all day would get up at night to begin again; who found the cure of all diseases, including indigestion, in more abundant eating.

I paid my compliments to Vlas' food, his great capacity and to his size.

"Huh!" said the old man, shaking his head sadly. "What I might be now if it hadn't been for the Revolution!"

This pre-Revolutionary *Papasha*—as he was called by daughters and sons-in-law—became the subject of half-boasting, half-bantering comment.

"Luckily *Papasha* didn't fall in with Bri-kovka peasants in the hunger year," said son-in-law Lukas, the tar and rope trader, "he would have made a month's meat supply for the village."

"Or turned into candles, he would have lit the churches till Ilya's Day," said son-in-law Feodor, the cloth merchant.

"*Papasha* doesn't like the Revolution, but he might have died long ago if there had been none." This from younger daughter Lina.

To her remark I gave point, by citing cases of people saved from untimely graves, thanks to the work, hunger and rigors imposed on them by the Revolution. There was Madame Rim-sky-Korsakov of S. In the old days she rose at noon full of ailments, a hardship to walk around her boudoir. The Revolution took away her money and gave her six people to help support. Now she is up before dawn, dragging great sacks of black bread and potatoes back from the bazaar, four versts away. The troubles of others give her no time to dwell on her own.

Then the old epicure, the landlord I met on a Volga steamer. In the old days of high living, he had catarrh of the stomach and half the doctors of Germany prescribing for him. The Revolution took away his delicacies and put him on a diet of black bread and cabbage soup—when he could get them. "The best specialist was the Revolution," said he. "It gave me a stomach that digests nails."

Vlas, it would seem, was another example of the saving power of the Revolution, fear and famine frying off great slabs of the fat that was smothering and choking him. All this to Vlas, of course, was sheerest nonsense, as ridiculous as making the sign of the cross with three fingers instead of two. To him food and fat are good things in themselves—the more the better.

Indeed, his chief grievance it seems against the Revolution was not for the six expropriated *datchas*, or the three hundred poods of tallow, the six hundred poods of salt beef it took out of his cellar, but for the four poods of fat it took off his belly. His set aim is to win it back, and the old man beams satisfaction at his growing circumference making progress on the road to "recovery."

"More vodka!" cried Vlas. Out of big jorums he kept the red and white vodka gurgling, drinking with each guest in turn, and when he had drunk everybody full, drinking by himself—twenty tumblers. The only apparent effect of it all was to liven up his legs and set him capering across the floor snapping his fingers.

I complimented him on the nimbleness of his legs.

"Yes," said Vlas, slapping them. "Woolen stockings on them all summer and they never sweat or stink. I got them as captain of my ship on the Volga."

"You mean your uncle's old barge," scoffed Shura.

Passing this over, Vlas resumed: "My grandfather lived to be a hundred and sixteen years."

"One hundred and six!" put in Shura.

"Well, one hundred and ten," conceded Vlas.

"Hundred and six! and not a year longer."

Vlas sullenly capitulated. Shura always puts a blight on his stories. When she is absent his grandfather grows to be one hundred and twenty-six. His own one thousand *verst* journey to the Kirghiz becomes three thousand. Ten thousand horses were frozen to death before his eyes. His broken leg hung by the skin like a hinge. Like "Lightnin'," who boasted that he drove a swarm of bees across the American continent without losing a bee, Vlas' tales have sweep and imagination.

But none of this when Shura is around. Besides an irritation arising from a too close and constant conjugal life, Shura harbors against Vlas an incident of long ago. She was not consulted about her husband. He was picked out by her father as was the procedure in those days. Not on that score does she base her grievance. But on her wedding night some one knowing Vlas' weakness, came and cried into the bedroom window.

"Eh, Vlas! A big wall-on-wall fight in the next village!"

"And the good-for-nothing," said Shura with terrible venom, "jumped into his clothes, fought all night and didn't come back till morning."

"Yes," said Vlas sheepishly, "and it's been eating her for forty-two years. When she's buried she'll still be talking about it."

"I ran home," continued Shura, "but my father beat me with a halter, and drove me back. If I had said anything my husband would have beaten me with his fists. But those days are over. They don't dare do that any more."

"More's the pity," commented Vlas gloomily. "The Revolution has spoiled everything—even the women. In the old days women used to weep at weddings. Now it's the men."

But Vlas' rancor against the Revolution for

putting rebellion into Shura is softened by the fact that at the same time it has made her an economic asset. In the new land code, the wife has equal claims to the land with the husband. To Vlas' two dessyatines of orchard are added the two that are Shura's in her own right.

This orchard is Shura's great wide *terem*. Majestic, strong featured, with a soft blue cashmere shawl pinned under her chin, she looks the *boyarina* one sees so often in the Moscow opera. Here all summer from dawn to dark she is pruning and scraping and spraying her beloved trees.

"*Mamasha* is so much in the orchard," said daughter Lina, "that she looks like it. Her hair is as white as the spring blossoms and her cheeks are as red as the autumn apples."

"She doesn't ever go to the theater," said Vlas approvingly. "The nightingales and cuckoos are horns and balalaikas to her."

This was Vlas' one poetic outburst. His own approach to the orchard is highly practical. Pulling down a branch he counts the little green knobs, calculates the number of poods the tree will bear, and puts a corresponding number of leaves in his pocket. At last the leaves all laid out and counted he announces, "As she stands two hundred barrels, one thousand rubles!"

A record crop this year. But apples are an uncertain quantity. Next year there may be none at all. So Vlas doesn't depend only on his apples. He is a cereal expert. His season begins when the first wagons come creaking in from the villages laden with the first offerings of the grain-fields.

Along the lines of peasant wagons moves Vlas. Down goes his arm deep dredging into an open sack. Up it comes with a bursting handful. He sniffs it, hefts it, tosses it, sifts it, then cries out: "116," "130," "132," figures defining the quality of grain. He can do it with his eyes shut and never make a mistake.

"I never cheat a peasant and they never cheat me," Vlas asseverates solemnly.

"How is that?" I ask him.

"I knock them down when they try it—or at least I did before the Revolution."

This is not an idle boast, for there are authentic stories of Vlas in the old days cleaning up half the bazaar.

In those days Vlas was a buyer for private traders, speculators and merchants. Now individuals have been replaced by institutions. Now the log elevators standing like block houses along the river front flaunt the signs Bread Products, *Gosbank*, *Goob Coop*. Now Vlas is a "red merchant" buying for the Coöperative—a huge impersonal corporation. He can't bargain with it, nor joke and drink vodka with it as he did with his former masters. Vlas misses that. But it doesn't affect the zeal and energy and conscientiousness of his work.

He is the oldest buyer in the market, but the most active. When the grain sledges cross the frozen Volga, Vlas is up before dawn to meet them. When the red flag goes up on the central *kiosk* announcing the opening of the market, Vlas, with all the gusto of an old wall

[43]

fighter, plunges into the thick of the buying, his great globe body rolling in and out among the sledges, puffing, shouting, scolding, joking, chiding. This is Vlas' element: food in the raw, food in abundance, mountains of it, chuting into elevators, filling the barges—food going out to feed the world. And Vlas is part of the process. The joy of it shines in his face. It exalts. It intoxicates. It transfigures him.

On these big grain days a veritable revolution is wrought in his property-loving soul. The crass old individualist is socialized. "My orchard," "my house," gives way to "our wheat," "our Russia," "our coöperative."

"Look what our coöperative has given me!" he cries, digging a paper out of his pocket and reading: "In recognition of faithful services performed by Vlas Alexsevich Podkletnov."

"See!" says the old man. "There's the seal. There's the sickle and hammer!" The same pride as a Red Armyist in his Service Medal.

"You know our country is great," Vlas goes on. "In the Kuban the crop ripens a month earlier than here. They talk of ordering me down there this season. Anywhere they send me I'll go, even to America. But they wouldn't let me in, would they? They would say I'm a Bolshevik."

Old Believer Vlas arrested as a Bolshevik! His great carcass heaves with laughter. Suddenly he stops, saying:

"But I'm just like a Communist. I've got a red card. I'm a Union man." He shows me a tiny red book certifying his membership in the Union of Soviet Employees, and recounts its privileges: Nine rubles a month out-of-work benefit; forty rubles at the birth of a child; free medicine.

"But what good is that to me?" says Vlas regretfully, "I'm never out of work, never sick and my *baba* is too old for babies."

Vlas, however, is a good Union man. Dues paid to date, not a black mark on the pages for reprimands and reproofs, and on Soviet holidays Vlas always in the front ranks near the tribune, his good right ear glued to the speaker.

[45]

Maybe he can get a clew as to what the Revolution was about. To what purpose it took away his *datchas*, beef and tallow, his Falstaffian figure and the spirit of obediance that once was Shura's. Another grievance against the Revolution is that it loosed on him bandits and bourgeois-baiters. Though he tried hard to make himself inconspicuous, his nine poods too magnificently incarnated their conception of a *bourzhôey*, and made him the target for their terror, rapacity and humor.

One night robbers came demanding five thousand rubles. On his refusal they led him down to an ice hole in the Volga, saying: "Pray your prayers, old man, then down the river under the ice to Astrakhan!" A hundred times he crossed himself, then turned to find the bandits had vanished.

Another time a saber was flashing above his head. "Shall I carve him?" asked the swordsman. "No! He's a full blooded old devil. Too big a mess he would make."

Again he was whisked away from his samovar to run the gauntlet of the Red Chambers. Four rifles blazed at him in the dark and he fell unconscious. Coming to, Vlas felt about for blood and holes in himself. There were none. It was a hoax with blank cartridges.

Naturally enough, these memories rankle in his breast, and occasionally smoldering resentment flashes into fire. But he tries valiantly to let bygones be bygones, to forget and forgive. All in all, the old man is a remarkable case of adaptation to the new system of life and ideas.

One thing that helps reconcile Vlas to the new order is that, to Vlas, as to all sectants, the Revolution means freedom in religion, a release from the persecutions with which the State Church hounded them since 1665. It exiled them to the far off forests and wastes of Russia. It confiscated the treasures out of their churches. It broke up their monasteries down on the Irtish River. It closed their asylums and divinity schools. It fell on them with fire and sword.

It is noteworthy that the Communists have used no measure against the Orthodox State

[47]

Church that that church has not used for centuries against the non-conforming faiths. In fact, it went far beyond anything the Communists ever attempted. No slanders were too base, no cruelties too vicious.

The Old Believers were declared a menace to the state and put outside the law. Their nostrils were ripped by pincers. Their children were made bastards and torn from their parents. Seals were put upon their altars and gates, their clergy were forbidden to perform their offices. More than once Vlas has brought a priest at night, disguised as a merchant, to conduct worship. And to ward off a raid on his church Vlas often carried hush money to the police.

One time the Procurator charges "a serious crime against Old Believers of Kvalinsk for the ringing of bells from their belfries, thus luring and tempting citizens to attend their services, a scandal not permitted in Saratov or Kuzentzk." Orders were issued by the Governor to muffle the bells.

[48]

The Revolution of 1905 took the seals off the altars. The Revolution of 1917 gave them equal rights alongside of the other faiths. With right of assembly, they used to convene in Kvalinsk a unity council of three branches of the Old Believers. Hither came three hundred delegates out of Old Moscow, out of the forests of Archangel, the valleys of the Caucasus and the Caspian steppes—out of the Russia of far away and long ago. Had I not known Vlas, I would have wondered how this strange, weird assembly of figures could have survived the Revolution. Big, hulking merchants who might have stepped out of the marts of Old Novgorod. Gaunt hollow-eyed monks who might have stepped down out of the ikon frames. Priests with fanatic devotion to the ancient ritual, like their forefathers ready to be burnt to death for it and equally ready to burn others.

"A foreigner! A spy!" thundered at me a giant virgin-bearded Cossack of the Don. "Put him out!"

[49]

They did so. But old Vlas smuggled me in again. And in course of time they grew tolerant of me. I even lured one of them, a Siberian priest, to my house. Five goblets of wine and the pent-up hatred against the old State Church broke out in a flaming tirade:

"Snuff pinchers! They make the sign of the cross with thumb and two fingers. Cowards! They couldn't compete with the true faith and put seals on our altars. Liars! They founded their religion on deceit. So they betray everybody, even those who confess to them. Why, if some one confessed to me that he killed the Tsar, it would be my secret forever. Police spies, charlatans, wolves. . . ."

In contrast with such extremists Vlas is a modernist and has departed far from the faith of his fathers.

The strictest Old Believers will not touch tea or sugar, nor potatoes, for they were unknown before the days of Nikon. But to Vlas all food is good.

The strictest Old Believers, holding that

false religion defiles a man in body and soul, keep themselves sternly aloof from the "worldly" and unclean. In the villages, zealots often refused to shake the hand I proffered and the bowl I ate from—as I found later—was the one from which the cat was fed. Any other dish I defiled would have to be broken or thrown away. When I told Vlas of this he only laughed and to prove that he had no such prejudices made me drink from the same bowl with him.

The Revolution has done much damage to Vlas' observance of the ancient customs and conventions. Even for those to which he conforms he gives secular and not religious reasons.

The strictest Old Believers lay no razor to their face, for the beardless may not enter heaven. Bandits once waylaid Old Believers with the demand, "Your money or your beard!" If the beard was severed it was gathered up to be buried with its owner lest at the gates of Paradise he be unrecognized. When I asked Vlas why he doesn't cut his whiskers off, he shook his head and said: "Do I want to look like a dog?"

The strictest Old Believers use no tobacco. It was unknown before Nikon and the Scriptures say: "Not what entereth into the mouth, but what cometh out, defiles a man." Vlas bases his abjuration of smoking on purely physiological grounds. It will cut down his weight. "Do I want to look like a weasel?"

To Vlas sheer size and bulk are virtues in themselves. He is proud of his big self, his big daughters, his big ikons, his big cross with the legend *"Vladika!* Ward off my enemies." Proudest of all of his enormous *Nomakanon*, the laws and Scripture in archaic red and black Slavonic script. To Vlas a magic spell lies in its great dimensions, in its great age—more than three hundred years he boasts. The very reading of it has a healing power.

This Vlas was doing in a loud voice when I came to say good-by. The room oven-hot, the ikon lamps a-lit, a sizzling samovar, haunches of pork and beef and pies on the table, and the old man—barefooted, in his black *kaftan*, vodka pouring into him, sweat pouring out of him—was sing-songing a prayer out of his holy book.

"Just curing myself of a cold," said Vlas apologetically.

Good health to Vlas! Hoch to Vlas!

Maybe long after the ascetic Bernard Shaw has finished his meatless, wineless days, this voracious flesh-eating, vodka-drinking, Bible-reading, union-carded Old Believer will continue to stand a bulwark of his ancient faith, refuting all laws of physiology and hygiene and some of the tenets of Marxism.

III
THE VALLEY OF WINE

III

THE VALLEY OF WINE

On a clear May morning we started out on the highroad that runs east from Tiflis. Behind us lay the "stony girdle of the globe"—so the Caucasus was known to the ancients—sending its white peaks high up to mingle with the white clouds of the summer sky. Before us in the distance were peculiar clouds of another color. Here and there along the highroad they rose in columns, now standing still, now moving slightly toward us—big, billowing clouds of dust. I had been reading local history, and beneath these rolling clouds I could see the Persians riding to sack the Georgian cities, the Golden Horde, in its migration from Asia into the West, and Timur the Tatar.

But nothing so frightful and fantastic. It was the spring migration of the sheep to the mountains. In hundreds of thousands they came—one, two or three thousand in a flock—headed by a big, important buck and assistant he-goats showing the way and flanked by weary-eyed dogs and shepherds. Out of the hot, blazing valley they follow this road that leads to the hill trails and up to the cool springs and succulent grass of the mountain meadows. Into rich pasturage, but into no shepherds' paradise. For up there are avalanches, hailstorms and wolves—and worst of all, there are the sheep raiders. The story of last year's raid we heard from a passing shepherd.

"We had moved up into dangerous passes," he said. "But the night was pitch-dark, and we were well hidden in the hollows. So we felt safe. Suddenly at midnight a flame shot from a cliff. It was a rocket. Another and another followed until the whole mountain was alight. There was gun-firing, yelling, the rush of a hundred horsemen. We were all bound and gagged and our sheep driven off—six thousand of them. All that was left for us was the spring's shearings and fifty skins of sheep-cheese."

It would have been interesting to follow the sheep—slow-moving avalanches of wool going up the mountains. But Arakel, my companion, said, "No, we must hold to our goal," and Arakel generally has his way. Between his big bushy beard and big bushy astrakhan cap blazed a pair of snapping eyes, quick as his lithe body, compelling as his will. That will had been tempered in furnace and field, by flogging and Siberian exile, by sixty years' fighting for freedom. Now, as if in compensation for the youth it robbed him of, the Revolution had given him a pension and turned him out to play. He was free to go whither his fancy took him.

To-day it was taking him into Kakhetia, into the Valley of Wine.

There was a foretaste of that valley in the red and amber vintages of the goatskins sold along the way at a ruble or two a skinful. The emptied skins were left at the next station for refilling. Omar dreaming of his body after death wrapt in winding-sheet of vineleaf, how he must have envied those goats so graciously fated to have their skins filled again and yet again. The old Persian must have had these Georgian neighbors in mind when he wrote his verses.

For wine runs in the Georgian's veins. Along with his mother's milk he gets his father's wine. Everywhere one sees fruits of the vine and the vine itself. Even over the façades of churches it climbs chiseled in stone, funny-faced lions blandly munching at the grapes. And the most sacred relic in Georgia, the cross the Virgin Mary placed in the hand of Saint Nina as she slept, is appropriately a grape-vine. Nina herself is buried in her convent at Signakh—the gateway to this Valley of Wine.

From here our road ran through fifty versts of vineyards—tendrils and leaves all in brilliant early summer green—a sight moving the old Georgian with us to philosophic comment. "Nature," he said, "by soil and climate apportions a nation its beverage as she does its food. Just as beer is ordained for Germans and *kumiss*, or mare's milk, for the nomads of Kirghiz steppes, so wine is the natural drink of the Georgians." Otherwise why did the grapes grow here so gloriously? Could any one answer that? No one could. Thereupon the company untied the leg of another goatskin and drank to the good fortune that placed them here in Georgia, where wine runs out of the soil.

Redder still is the fluid that has run into this soil. Every pass and hill and highroad has for centuries been soaked in blood. Twenty times, big armies have penetrated into this Valley of Wine, burning and plundering, robbing it of everything but its beauty. This warring past is reflected in the crumbling ruins of forts that crown the heights. It shows itself in the dress of the peasants—across the breast runs a row of cartridge-pockets and from the belt hangs a silver *kinjhal*, or poniard. It is in the greeting that Arakel flings to the men who line up as we drive through the gate at Tsinindal.

"Be victorious!"—"*Gaumerjabo!*" he cries out.

"And may the victory be yours!"—"*Gaumerjos!*" rings back the gallant answer.

Despite their warlike words these men are not warriors going forth to battle. They are vine-growers, very peaceful and poor. Rather, they *were* poor until the Revolution came and gave to each his "norm" of vine-growing land. Thus it came about that all had wine to sell. But they got so little for it—five cents for a bottle that in Tiflis sold for fifty cents. A hundred bottles for a pair of boots. So they became traders themselves, founding a coöperative, which any one might join by bringing in ten *vedros*, two hundred bottles.

To-day is the first big meeting. The officials are down from Tiflis. Interest is at high pitch. The big cool aromatic shed is crammed to the doors with all manner of men, ranging from ex-Prince Chavchavadze to his ex-lackey and the one-time village beggar. But now there is neither prince nor pauper. "All toiling peasants." All coöperators.

At one end was a great trough, where last fall in shifts of day and night, knee-deep, they tramped out the grapes with their feet.

"Primitive!" I exclaimed.

"Yes," said Arakel, who, though a modernist, has always a good word for the old. "But in one way feet are better than machines. They press out only the sweet juice of the grapes without the bitter juice of the stems." He pointed out the course of the juice piped from the big troughs into enormous jars set in the ground and tamped down with earth.

Above this lake of wine the meeting is called to order. It runs like a well-oiled machine. And so it is. For a flying battalion of Com-

munists has arrived and in caucus has fixed the
procedure in advance. Everything goes according to program: the report on last year's gains,
the fight against phylloxera by the grafting on
of American roots, the donation of six hundred
rubles for water-supply. All this proceeds
amidst a drum-fire of oratory praising the peasants as "arbiters of their destiny," "creators
of a new world," congratulating them on their
"initiative," "independence."

Are these merely words and phrases? So it
seems. For the only part these peasants take
in the proceeding is to chorus "Yes! Yes!"
to all proposals of the officials. Compliments
apparently suffice to make them docile. So the
machine slips along smoothly until it comes to
the election of three directors at salaries of one
hundred fifty rubles a month. For these posts
three Communists have been slated. But no
sooner are their names read than, in a withering blast from the benches, breaks a hurricane
of "No! No! No!"

The machine stops dead, and there is no

starting it again. Finally an old blind peasant gets the floor and says: "Now it is the custom to praise the peasants as in old days it was to abuse us. They used to call us sheep, and there is a lot of truth in that. We are a big flock going one way because others are going that way too. But the sheep don't pick their own path. It's the goats that show them. The directors are the goats. If the goats lose their heads and go over the cliff, the sheep follow them. On the other hand, sure-footed goats lead the flock up into good pasturage. Much, very much, depends upon the leaders. Let us see that we choose wise ones."

More speeches follow and at last the sense of the peasants expresses itself thus: "We will take one Communist, because he will make it easier to deal with the government. But the other two directors must be our old specialists: men whom we know and who know their business." The Communists, be it said, know a storm when it blows, and they bend to it. So it is ordained, and so it is voted. Then seven peasants are elected to look after the directors, and the assembly files out of the building, sniffing various savory smells now exhaling from the yard. A feast is now the order of the day.

The Georgian is by nature addicted to feastings. His life is an almost unbroken series of them. His christening, his marriage, his advent into this world, his going out—all are hailed by special feasts. Even when he lies moldering in the grave, his friends meet on three different occasions and solemnly gorge themselves in his memory. There are feasts to celebrate the spring sowing, the autumn reaping; feasts in honor of horses and cows, in honor of worms that they may be merciful to the crops, in honor of birds that they may be merciless to the worms. In the autumn comes a week's festival for Saint George. All the other saints are fêted, likewise all the great church holidays. Now come the six new holidays of the Revolution. The Georgian greets them with a cheer. Six new occasions for a feast.

To-day was an especially glorious occasion. So, while the meeting was on, the fires had been blazing in the big brick oven, and the steam, in fragrant columns, had been rising from the bubbling caldrons. Now the peasants told off as waiters were unrolling cylinders of linen across the grass, striping the green meadows white. The company, doubling up its plastic Asiatic legs, sat down, and presently the cloths were strewn with bundles of pungent grasses and cresses and armfuls of *choorek*, or Caucasian barley bread. We had seen this bread in the making. In the bottom of a big tiled kiln set in the earth a fire was kindled. Around the inside of the kiln was plastered the dough, which the hot air-blasts, rising from the bottom, quickly turned into bread.

"Rather primitive," I had again remarked to Arakel.

"Yes, but good bread," he rejoined. "I set

[67]

up in my house a modern stove with a closed oven. In a month my wife made me take it out. She said she liked bread baked in the old way, in the free air, not in a prison."

It was indeed most admirable bread. It served us not only as food but as a plate and napkin. With it too we handled the lamb now served up in various guises. First it came as soup seasoned with a strange herb. Then out of the caldrons it came as stew, and out of the oven roasted. Each form seemed more delicious than the other. I extolled the Georgian cooks for their skill in bringing out the essential flavors of the lamb.

"And you may praise the good grass of the mountain meadows for putting the flavors into it," said one feaster.

"And the good air," said another.

"And the good view," added Arakel quite seriously.

This was the first time I had heard that animals were affected by scenery, and I said so.

"Not only lambs," asseverated Arakel solemnly, "but all animals. My goats, for example. I just cut through an opening that gives them a wide outlook. At once they showed their appreciation."

Further tributes to the esthetic nature of lambs were warmly paid by the two mountaineers at the left—holding up a lamb-leg on their daggers. Little benefit the lambs got out of the eulogies. The gorging went steadily on. It is hardly correct, however, to say that the Georgians gorge themselves. Their feasts are rather more like a drowning operation. They are founded not on bread and meat but on wine. Holding that there is nothing to buy half so precious as the stuff they sell, these vintners devote a goodly portion of their products to themselves. The Georgian admires his wine and wants you to admire it too. You best can praise it by drinking it.

The chief drinker was the old landlord, Shakro. He was the pride of the valley, having met the heavyweight drinkers from all parts and drunk them all down. His record at one sitting was an incredible amount—some thirty or forty bottles—contradicting all the known laws of inner expansion. In his stomach must lie the secret of the fourth dimension. He saved himself from bursting by a girdle that encircled his enormous waist like a barrel-hoop. In fact he resembled nothing in this world so much as a barrel.

It was a prodigious feat to hold the title of champion in such a company—for they were all noble drinkers, and their insatiable thirst kept the tankard-carriers on the run, dipping the wine out of the cisterns, bringing it dripping across the grass and pouring it into vessels of varied shape and form, also made out of the local soil. Among them was a peculiar cup such as only a Georgian might devise. Into it ran a tube from another cup. Thus, while appearing to drink a single cupful, in reality one drank two. Likewise there was a flagon with a quaintly twisted neck, the favorite of the old patriarch, who sat opposite me. With a free swing of the arm he flung it above his head and kept it tilted there as the contents with gratifying sound gurgled first through the long neck of the flagon and then down his own throat. He drained it as if it were a tumbler. Once I tried to interrupt the process with the offer of a cigarette. He took it with his free hand, first touching my wrist with a light, graceful motion —the way the Georgians have for saying "Thank you" wordlessly—but not for a second did the steady downpour of liquor stop.

In this feat he was ably accompanied by his cronies on the right and left. They finished their flagons; then, as is the wont of an older generation, they began to berate the rising generation for departing from the way marked out by their fathers. Specifically the grievance against the young was their disregard of ancestral drinking codes and customs. The rising generation did not drink enough.

"Look around you," said the first old patriarch. "There are a dozen young fellows who haven't finished a single tankard yet."

"And my nephew comes home with loose talk

about too much wine wrinkling up the liver,"
snorted the second. "As if I hadn't fed my
liver wine for seventy years."

The third dwelt at length upon a scandalous
situation that was developing. Things had
come to such a pass, he averred, that the young
fellows, about a hundred of them, had actually
made a compact to limit themselves to a bottle
a day—a very bad omen, boding no good for
the future.

"In America," I interjected consolingly, "a
bottle a day—thirty bottles a month—would
be considered heavy drinking."

But they would not be comforted and continued to lament the decay of morals and drinking.

"And the reason for all this?" I inquired.

"Right there is one reason," said the first
old patriarch, blinking derisively at the pre-
siding officer of the feast—the *tamada*. The
tamada is a peculiarly Georgian institution.
He is elected by the assembly by virtue of the
prime qualities of his nerve, stomach and

tongue. His job is to put discipline into the feast and efficiency into the drinking. He must keep the wine and wit flowing. He must see that the goblets are filled to the brim and emptied to the bottom. He must be on the watch for those transgressing the rules of the feast and prescribe the penalties. Woe to the culprit who lags a bit behind in his cups! The tamada, spying him out forthwith, presents him with a big Caucasian ibex-horn, which the unfortunate laggard must drain at a draft. Such are some of the laws of the feast. To-day, however, they were largely in abeyance, and therefore was the ire of the older generation aroused.

But the tamada, if not strict in discipline, was eloquent in speech. He called the toasts:

"To the coöperators, who, throwing off a thousand years' guardianship of prince and landlord, have become their own guardians;

"To the revolutionary peasants, refusing to let others exploit their toil and by the same token refusing to exploit the toil of others;

"To Lado and Arakel, who from their childhood fought for freedom and now live to see their struggle crowned with victory."

These were toasts of the tamada. Then followed the toasts of the peasants, continuing long after the official feast was finished:

"To the Power now bringing peace amongst the tribes;

"To the Earth—out of it we mold these bowls and out of it we draw the refreshing wine we pour into them."

The wine often poured over the edges of the bowls and spilled upon the ground. I commented on this loss.

"Never mind, let the Earth drink too," was the answer.

Care enough they had taken in pruning, picking and treading the grape. Care-free they would enjoy the fruit of their labor. Give the Earth her libations too.

Many toasts were raised to Vermishev, once owner of the estate on which the coöperative stood, and to-day reëlected director: "To our comrade who found this land a hunting-place for bears and wolves and turned it into a garden. The work he began we promise to carry on."

"Remarkable the warm good-will of the peasants toward their one-time landlord," said I to Arakel.

But Arakel was not inclined to idealizing. "Good-will!" he gruffly interjected. "Why shouldn't they have good-will toward him? They've got his estates to divide among themselves. They've got his brains to run their coöperative. If anything is remarkable, it's the good-will of the landlords toward those who stripped them."

There was none who had been stripped more than ex-Prince Chavchavadze, the chief of the old nobility. The Revolution had taken from him honor, office and income. It had given him the pinch of hunger, the strain of unaccustomed toil. Worry and want had shrunken his huge body to almost half. But it was still an impressive figure; it still could flame with elo-

quence. The gist of his speech was in the clos-
ing words: "We had big estates. We held high
office. But were we happy then? No. Not
half so happy as we are to-day surrounded by
our peasant comrades."

It was a noble flight of feeling and apparently arose from deep within the man. Such a
fervor of fraternity must have swept that assembly of French nobles on the eve of the great
Revolution, when they declared their lands
forfeit to the people. History records that
they afterward repented of their rash bestowal
and fought valiantly in the counter-revolution
to hold their estates.

For just this reason Arakel was not impressed
by the rapture of Chavchavadze. "It doesn't
have any material basis," he explained. "To-
day he may have genuine emotions. But to-morrow he goes out into the fields. He sweats and
burns and itches. He thinks of the good old
days. He gets to longing for them. From this,
it's only a few steps to fighting for them. So
he is aways a possible counter-revolutionist."

In Arakel's opinion the one proprietor whose loyalty to the new order was on a sound economic foundation was Shakro. He is one of the ironies of the Revolution. He had poured his property down his throat until he became at last a landless landlord. Then came the Revolution with its slogan: "To each man the land that he can till." Shakro declared that he could cultivate two *dessyatines*, or about five and a half acres, and asked for it. The outraged Communists exclaimed that the Revolution came not to give land to the landlords but to take it away from them. Shakro stood by the letter of the law, however, the peasants stood with him and he came into his own again.

Now he sat smiling into his sixth tankard, surrounded by his rapt admirers and roaring out a song of glory to the Revolution. But, though his voice boomed up from his vast interior, big and resonant, it was lost in the choruses that broke out here and there or rolled together in thundering symphonies.

"Our music is all based upon the mountains,"

announced Arakel. "Like the main ranges, the main motives go steadily on. Listen and you will hear the tenors climbing the peaks, then coming back to . . ."

His fantasy was cut short by some one calling the toast: "To the sweet songs of Georgia and our fathers who wrote them."

Followed a song enchanting in melody and boundless in praise of Georgia. But reason enough for this extravagance of feeling. The scene before us was an extravagant loveliness. Across twenty versts of sloping fields, bright yellow with the mustard-flower, and old vine-yards, crimson with the poppy, we looked down to the silver Alazan, gleaming through its meadows. Then our eyes rose up to snow-crested summits hung now with the pink and purple mists of evening. No wonder that English devotee of Georgia, Wardrop, wrote: "It is more beautiful than anything I had ever seen or imagined."

But maybe he too was deep in Kakhetian wine—surely a magic draft. It not only made old men's voices soft and organ-like; hearts too under its spell became ever more expansive. With glowing affection a big mountaineer took me in his iron grasp and clutching me to his bearded bosom vowed eternal alliance between the two great powers—Kakhetia and America. This was the nearest approach to an act of violence that I saw the entire day. There was no unseemliness of word or gesture. It was an untarnished bacchanal of brotherhood.

We awoke next morning to a haggling dispute outside over bed and board and wages. But not a word about wine. The reason was quite simple. Wine being here regarded as a basic necessity, it is assumed that each workman gets as much as he wants.

As a protest against this unlimited consumption—Menik explained to us—had come the compact of the hundred young fellows, a sort of Georgian Young Men's Temperance Association, Limited—thirty bottles a month. "We don't say that wine in itself is bad; we simply say that too much of it is bad."

"But if wine is good, how can one get too much of it?" was the retort of the first old patriarch.

"But you know very well that they get too much wine. Only a month ago didn't two men die after a week's debauch?"

"Foolishness!" snorted the old man. "They got to sweating and, going to sleep in a draft, they both died from a cold. That's all."

Thus the debate went on, each man being called upon to declare himself—no neutrals tolerated. Arakel, though he belonged to the older generation, staunchly took sides with the young, going so far as to state that alcohol was "poison"—a very extreme position. But he held it valiantly, fortifying himself with frequent drafts from a goatskin.

Finally came my turn. As diplomatically as possible I broke to them the dreadful news that America prohibited vodka, whisky, gin, beer— and wine.

"Wine, too?" they repeated, dumfounded.

"Wine, too," I bravely reiterated.

When they revived from their shellshock, I went on to explain that America had eighty per cent of the automobiles of the world, likewise fifty per cent of the locomotives, sixty per cent of the elevators. It was one big machine, so that the fogging of the brain with alcohol, the trembling of the hand at the wheel or throttle, spelled disaster. A man's nerves must be steady.

"Steady nerves!" cried the old man in protest. "Well, let them drink wine. That's what it's for—to make the nerves steady."

To my skeptical smile he replied by pouring out a big bowlful and drinking it. Then a second and a third. Filling the fourth bowl to the brim, he placed it on his head, and, calling to me, "I'll show you," he stepped out into that wild, graceful dance of the Caucasus—the *lezghinka*.

Stamping the ground in ever faster measure, he suddenly unsheathed two daggers and, placing the tips of the gleaming blades on his eyes, launched out into the most complex figure.

I looked to see the daggers draw blood or the bowl fall shattering to the ground. One slight misstep or jerk would have done it. But nothing jerked except my own nerves. At last he came out of the dance, whirling like a dervish. With a fine gesture he stuck the two daggers into the table, placing the bowl between them. He nodded to me and laughed. It was as if he said: "There they are, three irrefutable arguments for drinking."

"Such a feat is beyond any American," I said quite truthfully. But the older generation would not allow my profuse compliments to divert them from their main issue. Their morale was fine after the signal exploits of their champion. In their glee was also an element of serious concern over the fate of America, going into a dry and sear decline. And they had an excellent example to hand—the Moslem. Many times I heard the argument: The Mohammedans once ruled Asia. They penetrated into Europe. They were as power-

ful as America. But they drank no wine.
Where are they to-day?"

"If Mahomet hadn't forbidden wine, we
might all be Moslems ourselves," said one of
the vine-growers. "They sacked our cities.
They wasted our land. They did convert certain tribes—the Ossetins. But we clung to our
faith and wine."

But what Mahomet failed to do with the
sword the Communists essay to do with the
word. A profane and sacrilegious crew. They
have invaded this very Valley of Wine with
crude posters picturing a Georgian gagged and
bound by alcohol. Beneath are the words:
"Wine weakens will, mind, body"; "Out of
the taverns into the schools."

Outrageous blasphemy to these votaries of
wine. Our guide looked at the poster and past
the vineyards rolling down for forty miles.
Then, pointing out a tavern across the way, he
said, "There's a good place to get a round of
drinks."

IV

IN THE VILLAGE OF SALVATION

IV

IN THE VILLAGE OF SALVATION

AGAIN I am on the road that runs over the Vladimir hills to the village of Salvation. It was Yanyshev who first led me here, in the fateful summer of 1917. He is dead now. So are thousands of his comrades. So are millions of other Russians, who perished of bullets and hunger and horror in the revolutionary hurricane that swept the land, changing institutions and ideas to their foundations, changing the very course of history.

Yet, with all these changes, one has no sense of change here. All is quite as it was on that summer day years ago. The same creaking cart; the same wayside talk about cattle and crops and plagues of grasshoppers; the same wide billowing waves of wheat sweeping away to the horizon; and out of these green seas, like great white cliffs, the same white churches lifting their blue and gold domes above the huts of the villages clustering around them. From a rise in the road, six years ago, I counted twenty-four of these churches. But to-day the air is clearer, and I can count thirty-six, standing sentinel across these plains that bear the name of Vladimir.

It was this Vladimir that first brought Christianity to Russia a thousand years ago. A colored lithograph of that historic event hangs in almost every peasant's hut; the half-naked, half-savage Slavs stand waist-deep in the water of the Dnieper, while Saint Vladimir baptizes them into the Orthodox faith.

How well these Slavs have kept the faith, nurtured it and lavished on it their wealth, bear witness these great edifices that capture the eyes with form and color and pour the music of their bells into the ears, intent on dominating the mind as they dominate the landscape. They stand there so massive, so enduring, so unchanged by the revolutionary storm.

Is the faith they enshrine unchanged? How has it weathered the gale?

I would have put these questions to the old priest of Salvation village. But he had passed on. And when we knocked on the door of the parish-house it was a new priest, a tall fair-haired Slav of thirty-five, who invited us in with a smile. It was a somewhat anxious smile. For why should a Communist and an inquisitive stranger from America appear in this little far-away village? But he could not long harbor suspicions. He was too amiable by nature. And there were other excellent reasons for being good-natured.

Six months earlier, in a neighboring village, he had been the teacher, "Popov." Then he had been ordained a priest and become "Little Father" (*Batushka*) Popov. And, by marrying the daughter of the old priest of Salvation parish, he had at once secured a pretty and capable wife, an excellent house and garden, and a parish whose revenues were not deeply cut into by the currents of anti-religion.

Being seated, the Communist felt impelled forthwith to introduce some anti-religion into the young priest's mind: "How could all the animals have gotten into the ark?" "Where did Cain get his wife?" "Why do the atheist peasants of France get bigger crops than the religious peasants of Russia?" and similar assaults upon the foundations of the faith. The young priest was as awkward in religious controversy as in the new gown in which he was robed. He amiably and disgracefully yielded point after point, taking a stand only upon the Doctrine of Holy Water. But it was a firm stand.

"Take two bottles," he explained to me, as an outsider. "Fill one with just ordinary water. Fill the other with water that has been blessed in the proper way. Let them stand a few months—the ordinary water may be spoiled, but the consecrated water will be just as fresh as new."

"Did you ever do that experiment?" asks the Communist.

Father Popov was quite dumbfounded. For to him, as to tens of millions of members of the Orthodox Church, this is as plain matter of fact. This is the way water acts. Heat water and it boils; freeze water and it solidifies into ice; consecrate water and it stays unspoiled. What is there to experiment about? And how can you argue with a person who does not even know the common properties of water?

Father Popov was exasperated. His mild voice was rising in irritation when a voice from the kitchen diplomatically called him out to fix the samovar. Returning evidently with fresh instructions from his wife, who, as a priest's daughter, was better versed in ecclesiastical and parochial matters, he evaded further debate, valiantly confining his talk to his garden, his orchard and his hives. Even the Communist's jeer against Beneficent Deity putting stings into bees and worms into apples failed to lure him into further argument. He stolidly refused to justify the ways of God to a Communist.

His wife meanwhile laid the table, proud of her white linen but apologetic for lack of white bread. "Last year the worms ate the wheat all up," she said. "They ate it up in the fields just as it was ripening for the harvest; the grasshoppers and worms came in armies."

"And to-morrow," said the young priest, his native good humor once more asserting itself, "there is to be a procession around the fields of the east village. There will be a special service against all these plagues. If you would like to go with us, come along. Please come along!"

Next morning we wake to the tolling of the bells and slide down out of the hay-mow in time to see the procession forming in the church yard. The village elder is grumbling away:

"What is the matter, Ivan Mikhilovich? Where are the women to-day? Not even enough to carry the ikons!"

He shakes his head dourly. But the little girls are delighted. That means that they too will have ikons to carry. They stand eagerly, in pairs, before the church steps, and soon one of those great grave faces of the Saints, lacquered on board, is framed on either side by two shining-faced little girls. Little ikons for the little girls. Big ikons for the big girls. And last of all comes the wonder-working ikon.

"Careful! Very careful! Ivan Mikhilovich," cautions the village elder.

Why so careful? This is just another wooden lady with a wooden heart. So it seems. But once this wooden heart dripped blood. Struck by a careless hand, out of this unanimated board trickled real drops of ruddy blood. To prove the miracle, Father Popov points out the crimson stains, still visible. His morale to-day is greatly improved by the priestly garments in which he is swathed.

Adjusting the differences between the bearers of the Candle and the Cross, two mischievous young imps in black, he calls out to the standard-bearers. The men lift the banners, the bells break into a wild clangor, and the procession moves through the gates of the village and skirts the edges of the meadows.

East and west the grain fields roll away in rippling waves, their long leaves hung with dew-drops, their budding ears rich with the promise of life. But only the *promise*. Nine months these peasants have labored, plowing, scattering the seeds, watching the green blades push through the soil, growing up into stalks. Four weeks more and these green fields will stand brown and golden under the summer sun. Then harvest time, the russet sheaves, the beat of the flail on the threshing-floor—and bread for the coming winter. The life poured into the fields they shall reap again five-fold. *Maybe!*

For against these fields is camped an enemy, a ravaging, pillaging enemy. From all sides, creeping forward, flying the air, mining the earth, striking with fang and tooth and claw— armies of worms, hosts of caterpillars. That is why we go forth with banners to battle with the insects. Around these fields we are to-day to draw a magic circle. With cross and candle, prayer and holy water we are to build a barrier against ant and mouse and caterpillar. They shall not pass!

Let the earth blest by Thee bring forth fruit in its time. Allow not upon it any vermin, insect, rust, burning heat or withering wind bringing destruction. . . .

chants the priest.

Deliver us from our enemies!
Have mercy upon us,
Holy Triphon, pray for us!

respond the people.

"In the twentieth century!" exclaims the Communist reproachfully. "Just think. . . ."

But how can one think? The far-away voice of the church bell and the voice of the whispering wheat field, and the song of the lark, and the soft laughter of children mingle with the reverberant voice of the priest, reading, out of the Slavonic, a prayer which is poetry:

> Ye who created the skies and earth, who beautified the heavens with starry lights to shine upon the earth, and who adorned the earth with cereals and grass and various plants and flowers. . . .

Ten centuries slip away and I am back in the Middle Ages, walking in a solemn procession. Only this to-day is not too solemn. For the children, laughing, chase butterflies and pluck the buttercups and daisies; they twist them into chains to hang about their necks, or twine them into garlands for the ikons; the sun flashes back the silver of the robes and crosses; the golden banners wave above the women dressed in red and orange and brightest blue; and we move along the borders of the field—a caravan of color.

Four versts and we halt just where a brook, white with water-lilies, pours its heavy incense on the meadows. With faces and ikons looking to the altar-cross in the center, the people range into a circle and the service begins. It is a comprehensive service. First, general praise to the heavenly powers. Second, general exhortation to the people. Then it becomes specific. It calls up the third party, the cause of this procession. Their names are all written in the book. And the priest calls them out, naming them by name:

> Worms and grasshoppers!
> Mice and rats!
> Ants, moles and reptiles!
> Flies and horseflies and hornets!
> And all flying things that wreak
> Destruction . . .

he cries in a loud voice,

I forbid you in the name of the Savior come on earth to suffer for men. I forbid you in the name of the all-seeing cherubim and seraphim who fly around the heavenly throne, I forbid you in the name of the angels and the millions of heavenly spirits standing in the glory of God. I forbid you to touch any tree, fruitful or unfruitful, or leaf or plant or flower. I forbid you to bring any woe upon the fields of these people!

And the priest, dipping the *hyssop* (the long brush) in the water, raises it above his head and flings it until the drops fall a tiny shower upon the field, to the North, the South, the East and the West, and upon the heads of the people singing:

> Pray for us, Saint Triphon!
> Saint Triphon got the martyr's crown and died for Jesus.
> Holy Triphon, pray for us!

Surely, were there any pity or poetry in the soul of a worm, it could not spoil the fields of these poor folks, standing devoutly with bowed heads, trusting in the magic of these words come down through the ages. For these are not merely the words of their parish-priest.

They are the words of Saint Triphon, the martyr of Asia Minor, who, according to the chronicles, "The son of a poor peasant, from

babyhood loved the Almighty and under the
Roman Empire suffered death by steel and
fire." They are the words with which "in the
third century he delivered his land from the
plague of worms and insects, the destroyers
leaving forthwith at his command."

Now, after sixteen centuries, these peasants
of Salvation, in the voice of their priest, hear
the voice of the mighty Saint thundering to the
enemies of their fields this his IMPRECATION,
(as printed in the "Tchiti-minei" on page
179):

> If ye obey me not, meekest and humblest
> of God's servants, if ye leave not this place
> and go to arid mountains and sandy deserts,
> —then the God of Abraham, Isaac and Jacob
> will send by my prayer armies of birds to
> destroy ye. Ye shall perish by iron and lead.
> Ye will be caught and slain. By the Great
> Name written on stone, I adjure you! Like
> wax before fire, melt and disappear! Away
> from these fields! Away and perish!

Harsh, hard words. So unlike that gentle

Saint of Italy, friend to the lowliest of creatures, speaking softly to birds and worms and beetles he met along the way.

But Saint Triphon of Asia Minor is no Saint Francis of Assisi. He makes no appeal to the better nature of the worms. He believes only in their total depravity. He gives them no alternative but death. Death in far off wastes, or here in these green wheat fields. So harshly dealt with, shall they be blamed if they choose to perish in the succulent grain—and have the grain fields perish with them?

It is this hard fact that stares the peasants in the face. Despite the procession last year and the year before, it is not the insects, but their fields, that perish. And so the task of Saint Triphon grows harder. He has not only to drive the worms from the fields, but to drive the worms of doubt and disbelief beginning to gnaw at the hearts of the people. Else faith, too, shall perish. And much faith is needed, even to keep a procession marching under the heat of this midsummer day.

Hotter and hotter grows the sun. Heavier and heavier grow the banners. Sharper and sharper grow the corners of the ikons. And, like the flowers that hung upon the ikons, more and more wilted grow the spirits of the marchers.

Thus we come to an arm of wheat jutting out of the main fields like a promontory. There it is two long versts around it, but across just a few steps. How easy to take the short way across, flashes into every mind. All turn hopefully to the village elder to give the word. But he is not to be compromised. He only mumbles something about the long walk being very tiring to the children, and wearily mops his brow. But the banner-bearers, weighed with their heavy burdens, are more zealous.

"Strange, in this field there never were many worms," declares the first one.

"And it really isn't part of the main fields," says the second.

"Well, then, let's cut across it," blurts out Ivan Mikhilovich.

"Yes! Yes!" chime in a score of voices.

Only one, an old *baba*, objects. To her the point of ceremony is its exact and precise performance. In this lies its efficacy. No short cuts in the ritual, no short cuts in the marching. But she is overruled. Even the priest, perspiring under his heavy robe, is against her. And, moving forward, we are soon waist-deep in the waving sea of wheat, the priest atoning for his slight irregularity by vigorously flinging far out upon the uncircumscribed field generous portions of the holy water.

It is now almost all sprinkled upon the fields. The vessel is lighter, and so is the spirit of the village elder who carries it. He falls back for a little conversation.

"Ah, but you should have been here before the Revolution," he says. "Then everybody in the village took part. Those were real processions, like you must have in America."

I told him that in America we had no processions at all.

"No, really, is that so?" he exclaimed. "And

you have good wheat—lots of it. You sent it to our starving brothers on the Volga. I thank you for it." He took off his hat and bowed to me.

"Yes," I went on rather provokingly. "We raise crops, not by processions but by plows, deep-cutting plows and irrigation and chemical protection against insects."

"Quite so," he answered conciliatingly. "Maybe we ought to do more of that. That is what Fedosiev all the time is telling us. But he talks too much. Besides, he doesn't go to church any more. And he doesn't believe in the saints."

"Well, you believe in them," I continued cruelly, "but what good does it do? Does it really save your harvest from the worms?"

This thrust went too deep. He became grieved, almost hostile. Only after a long silence he went on to recount instances of harvests saved by processions. "If this fails to-day, it is because we fail. It is our lack of faith, God punishes us for our sins. Our village has grown indifferent and pleasure-loving."

And as if to point his homily, across the pasture came the shouts of the young fellows playing *gorodki*, the crash of the flying clubs, and the cry of the score at the top of their lungs.

This was too much for Ivan Mikhilovich. At best his piety was none too robust. And it was sorely strained by wrestling all day with a heavy banner.

"Devil take them!" he exploded. "We walk our legs off while these scoundrels play games, or sleep their heads off all day. And it's their wheat as much as ours. As for me, I swear never to go to a procession again—not until every man in the village goes too."

Boom! Boom! goes the big bell in the church tower. Tinkle! Tinkle! Tinkle! go all the little bells, awakening in unison to the sudden energy of the bell-ringer. It is like good music to our tired limbs. It sets our blood tingling. We pick up our step, and soon again are passing into the churchyard. The ikons and banner set up in their niches;

the cross is once more placed on the altar. Relieved of his sacred office, the young imp of a cross-bearer gives a good whack to the young imp of a candle-bearer, the girls call out good-bys to one another; and the young priest hurries home to break his long fast.

That evening I met Fedosiev and told him, by the way, about my pilgrimage of the day.

"So I had heard," he replied, "and I think none the more of you for it."

I have known Fedosiev a long time and he makes free to tell me what he feels. Not that he is rude or impolite. On the contrary, he is both in heart and manners a gentleman. Likewise a scholar. So alert, so wide in knowledge, so facile in expression. One would wonder at the miracle of the peasant Fedosiev, had not Tolstoy told us of such men in the "dark villages." "We should go to them and sit at their feet," he said, "they can be our teachers and prophets."

To his fellow-villagers, of course, Fedosiev seems anything but a prophet. He is just a peasant who goes away in the winter to work as a chimney-builder and brings back a lot of strange notions, extremely irritating to the older peasants. Insistently he points out the shame of Russia producing, per *dessyatine*, less than one third as much as Belgium or England. And he tells the peasants it is their shame, and calls them to cast off the old "grandfather ways." But with all his reformistic zeal, Fedosiev has much of the tolerance of the philosopher. I was surprised, then, to hear him in such dogmatic disapproval of the procession.

"But it was beautiful," I insisted. "It was like some ancient pageant of nature, a happy festival of the fields."

"For you, maybe," responded Fedosiev. "But not for the *mujiks*. They didn't take a day off in midsummer for a festival, or walk fifteen versts just to give themselves a good time. They did it for a definite purpose; to destroy the insects. It was an agricultural expedition. And, as such, it was sheer waste of energy. That isn't the way you raise wheat in

America. You don't frighten insects away from the crops with ikons, but spray them with chemicals. You don't sprinkle the fields with a bucket of water, you run great irrigation ditches into them. You don't wave banners above the fields, you put fertilizers into them."

"But as a procession, as a carnival, it was picturesque," I provocatingly insisted.

"Sorry you weren't around to help celebrate Frola and Lavra day," rejoined Fedosiev, a little ironical. "The peasants decorate the horses with ribbons and flowers and lead them past the priest to be sprinkled with holy water. In an epidemic they do the same—or used to. And it is all very picturesque. But when an epidemic kills off half the horses in the village, it isn't so picturesque. That isn't the way you treat a sick horse in America, is it? You don't stick a candle up before the ikons of Frola and Lavra. You take them to a veterinary, don't you?"

"You talk just like the Communists," I said, knowing that Fedosiev as a Left Socialist

Revolutionist had his own particular grievances against them.

"But here the Communists are right," he answered. "To make room for the new, a lot of the old must be blasted out. And the Russian *mujik* clings to his old ideas, his old customs, his old three-field system, his old way of putting things into the hands of the saints instead of taking things into his own hands. His *neechevo* (it doesn't matter) is just his old Asiatic fatalism. His orthodox religion is just his old heathenism dressed up in the Christian names. His so-called piety is just his old superstition and medievalism. Our villagers are a thousand years behind the times; look at the tree! That shows how deep we are in the Middle Ages."

He was pointing to one of the black-feathered trees, so characteristic of the village greens in this province of Vladimir. They are black feathered with multitudes of crows and ravens crowding their branches. They are so thick that one could not throw a stone without hitting a half-score of them. But that wouldn't even occur to a Russian. He would as soon think of stoning the village sheep as stoning the village ravens. The black flocks flying above the houses are as immune from harm as the white flocks nibbling the grass in the meadows. Freely the black-winged battalions maneuver through the air; now soaring down into a tree, and in a moment its glistening green becomes black; now lighting upon the church, turning the golden cupolas to soot. But these birds serve not only as an ornament of the trees and temples. They belong to the winged battalions with which Saint Triphon threatened the insects.

"True," says Fedosiev, "they destroy many of the pests, but still more they destroy the sprouting wheat and rye. They serve the *mujik* in the same primitive way as do our wooden plows and carts and *izbas*."

In Fedosiev's program the crows and ravens are likewise doomed to extinction. No longer will they wheel above the house-tops of the villages, flinging swift dark shadows on the ground. No longer, like the ancient Romans, will the inhabitants mark their comings and goings as signals and portents of the changing seasons. With the old ideas and old customs disappear much of the old beauty and charm and mystery.

"So much the less of poetry and romance in life," I assert.

"So much the more of wheat and sanitation, of schools and science," says Fedosiev.

V

COMRADE HARVEST

V

COMRADE HARVEST

I

"How are things in Russia?" I called out of the car window to the Red Army patrol at the Riga frontier. For answer he pulled out of his pockets two loaves and holding them aloft, waved them laughing. Bread, to him, was the symbol of prosperity.

With all workers and peasants I soon found it was the same. It was likewise the measure of value. Invariably into all our conversations would be injected the questions:

"How much is it a pound in America?"

"How many *poods* for an *arsheen* of cloth?"
By bread they sought to get at the real condi-
tions in America.

To the young giant striking north through
the Archangel forest with three fifteen-pound
loaves strapped to his back, bread was a measure of time. Usually, he explained, he told
time by the sun.

"But there is no sun. There's been none for
a week," I said.

"Then I tell it by the black bread in my
belly. When I eat one pound, I am hungry
in three hours. Two pounds, and in four or
five hours the worm demands to be fed." He
was a sort of human time-glass, with bread, instead of sand, running through him.

Most illuminating of all, the attitude of the
rain-drenched man in Samara taking refuge
from a June storm in my doorway. To my
condolences over his wetting he replied:

"*Neechevo! Neechevo!* (Never mind!)
This isn't rain. It is gold coming down from
the sky. It means bread for us all."

Where else in the world would a man with dripping clothes and chattering teeth dwell upon the social implications of the rain? Where else would he do anything, but curse it?

In such contacts I got an insight into the significance of bread in Russian life. It grew with my growing knowledge of the language. "Bread plowing" is the Russian word for agriculture. "Bread-bearing," the word for fertility. "Bread-bearer," another term for peasant. "Bread and salt," (*kheeb-sol*) means hospitality. Always I was finding new words for bread, the cereals from which it was made, the processes of its making. Sometimes the words came easily out of my dictionary. Sometimes painfully, as once on the lower deck of a Volga steamer.

While munching away at a chunk of bread, I was startled by a sudden cry of "Papa! Papa!" I looked up to see a baby stretching out his arms to me. By a stony indifferent countenance I sought to disavow my paternity before the public, and went on doggedly eating my bread. But the wretched child kept insistently repeating "Papa!"

With deep hatred I glared at the brat, and in turn felt the eyes of the passengers critically focusing on me. It went on, to my increasing discomfort, until suddenly the child wriggled out of his mother's arms, began crawling towards me. Cold sweat on my brow. The bread fell from my hands to the floor. The child grabbed it, and, holding it out to its mother, gurgled "Papa!"

Slava Bogoo! It was not me, but the bread that was *papa*, the curious name that the children give it all over Russia. The hostile glances of the public were not directed against me as a father disowning his offspring, but as a stingy man refusing bread to a hungry baby.

The Russian not only lavishes on bread every term of affection, he waxes lyrical over it.

> Only the golden wheat fields know
> The secret of their love.
> Stand up erect bright ears
> And hide the sweethearts true.

Thus goes on the favorite song of the village youth, *The Peddler* of Nekrasov. Bread appears in hundreds of songs and proverbs and in legends like this: "Fair and rosy did our Buckwheat grow. They invited her to visit Tsargrad. Off she set with Honorable Oats and Golden Barley. Princes and Boyars met her at the high stone gates. They set her on the oaken table to feast. As a guest has our Buckwheat come to us."

Not only in legends but in life bread receives homage as a personage. At the peasant's board it occupies the place of honor. Never must it be laid upon its side or top, always it must be placed upright. Thus, "Bread turns the table into an altar." The piece that falls upon the floor is picked up by a peasant who may even kiss it reverently. The children are warned that every crumb swept from the table means one less golden apple for them to pick in Paradise. Even the drops of *kvas* must not be tossed out of a glass, for it is made of bread. The loaf must be always cut to the right.

Some peasants will only break bread,—to cut it with a knife would be disrespect.

Not only the peasants pay honor to bread, but with bread they pay honors to others. It is in the hands of the relative welcoming the soldier home from the front. It rides at the head of the wedding procession. It is set on the table in front of the house as a tribute to the dead. With gifts of bread and salt the boyars greeted the tsars, and to-day, in the back villages, Kalinin is met by *mujiks* bringing him trenchers with these ancient symbols of hospitality.

The American says, "Give me the luxuries of life, and I can dispense with the necessities." When he prays, "Give us this day our daily bread," he means meat, eggs, cake and ice-cream. Not the Russian. He means literally bread.

"Six days without bread. Six days I starved!" exclaimed the skipper of a watermelon boat, ending his tale about the big storm that stranded him on a sand bar in the Volga.

"But you had some four thousand water-melons on board!" I pointed out.

"Yes," he added, "and we had fish and eggs. But no bread!" So he was starving.

If this seems far fetched, spread your table with the most ravishing dishes, but no bread. Then watch the eyes of your peasant guest constantly hunting about for bread. "Without bread," says the Russian proverb, "the palace is a prison. With bread, it is Paradise under a pine tree."

Bread is the only thing he cannot do without. In famine years a ten *pood* cow he will trade for two *poods* of flour.

II

Bread is the life of the Russian peasant. It is likewise the life of the Russian state. Hard bent are her statesmen in building the industries. But for decades yet her riches will come not from her iron and textile factories, but from her bread factories; not from the gold fields of Siberia, but from the vast grain fields, spreading a cloth of gold over the Russian land. In them reposes the might and power of the state. On them hangs the weal and woe of the nation.

"May the stalks be like reeds, the grain like peas and from every grain sown may we gather a thousand!" This prayer of the heathen Chuvash around the *kasha* kettle in the fields of Yeromkhin is the prayer of all Russians at the time of sowing. From the day the seed is put in the ground until the crops are gathered in, a close and anxious watch is kept upon it. Its general condition from infancy to maturity is telegraphed to Moscow from all parts of the country. Its symptoms are carefully diagnosed by specialists, like a board of consulting physicians, recording pulse, temperature and blood-pressure. Its state of health is daily bulletined by the newspapers, with space and captions worthy of the first citizen of the republic.

These bulletins begin in the fall with the sowing of the winter cereals:

Kharkov, October 10. Abundant warm rains are falling throughout the Ukraine, East of the Don and along the Black Sea Littoral.—Winter wheat stands at 5 balls.

Irkutsk, October 15. Continuous dry weather through Siberia had been extremely unfavorable and winter rye is rated as low as 2 balls.

Tambov, November 1. Heavy snow falling over the Central Districts had laid a protecting cover on the fields. All crops went under the snow at 3 balls.

In the five-ball system, the peculiar standard which Russians use in various fields, five means excellent, three average, one poor, etc. It is on this marking that the cereals are rated in the bulletins, even in their infancy and first early growth, until they disappear under the snow. But even then they do not disappear from the newspapers. Now there are bulletins upon the snow blanket and the cereals sleeping under it.

Odessa, November 10. Strong sun has

melted away the snow, leaving the fields exposed to freezing winds.

Smolensk, March 15. An early thaw followed by bitter cold has spread an ice film over the ground. Winter wheat which went under the snow at 3 balls is coming out at two.

As spring moves on into an early summer, the bulletins come thicker and faster, taking ever more space in the papers. The public watches the crop scores with the same keen interest that it watches the baseball scores on the boards in front of the big newspapers in America. Always there is a series of disasters to record. August frosts in Archangel, blighting the oats. Cloud bursts in the Kuban laying low the wheat, preventing its flowering. Floods on the Kama. Hail the size of duck's eggs in Vladimir. Ground fleas and pea-elephant in Yaroslav. Gophers and marmots in South Siberia.

All quite normal. It spells loss but not disaster. Only when some great scourge looms up does the public become tense and excited.

Then the bulletins take on the language of war. Bread, backed by all the resources of the Republic, fighting against the destroying forces. Thus in 1926 the battle is recorded:

THE GRASSHOPPER FRONT

Rostov-on-the-Don, July 15. The general situation in all sections is worse. Two new grasshopper armies are reported flying out of the Kalmik steppes. Favoring west winds expediting their advance. In the Terek the spring crops were decimated by the first army which is moving up on the right bank of the Volga.

Stavropol is declared in a state of siege. *Troikas* with extraordinary powers have been organized and all civil and military forces mobilized. Scouting aeroplanes and cavalry patrols are reporting new movements of the enemy. Special trains with the chemical command and anti-grasshopper "artillery" rushed to the Don section have been delayed by insect masses clogging the rails. Telegrams marked "Grasshopper" take precedence over all others. All efforts are concentrated on reaping the crops of the poor peasants.

Timaki, July 18. The orchards and gardens of the Kurort were saved by the heroic efforts of the workers in the Rest Houses and Sanatoriums. In readiness for the invaders, the people of Kabardoo were armed with pots, pans, scythes, stove screens. At the first sighting of the enemy in the sky, such a hellish noise was made by these instruments and the jangling church bells that they gave up their attempted landing and passed on.

The first army, bivouacking at night in the Volga meadows, attempted in the morning to cross the river, but was thrown back by great smoke curtains of burning straw and brush. In some places the fires were smothered by locust masses falling into them. The aeroplanes are hindered, in gas and arsenic spraying of cocoon breeding places, by the presence of people and cattle in the fields. Trenches have been dug on the borders of Stalingrad. The Kalmik Ispolkom has made heroic efforts to stop the flight of new hordes from the steppes. Under the pressure of unfavoring winds three armies are retreating to Dagestan. In the Kara-Kassak Oases the enemy has been liquidated.

At last the invaders are expelled. But behind them is a devastated area as big as Belgium. This same year there is drought in the Tartar Republic. Unprecedented hail lays an ice-coating a foot deep over tens of thousands of *dessyatines*. The Volga flood smothers two hundred thousand *dessyatines*.

Even so, 1926 is a banner year and the papers break out in extravagant cartoons of Comrade Harvest and Comrade Peasant dancing a roundelay of joy together. There is not enough twine and hemp to bind and bag the grain, not enough cars and elevators to carry and store it. So vast is Soviet Union it can well stand the shocks that would wreck a small country.

III

It is only when disaster is piled upon disaster that the catastrophe becomes nation-wide, and famine stalks over the land. This has

occurred in the history of Russia at not in-
frequent intervals and each time has left its
impression on the oral tradition.

Every epoch in which the country has been
stirred to its depths—the troubled times of
Boris Godoonov, Stenka Razin, Peter the
Great, Pugatchev—has brought forth a host
of curious tales and legends. The hunger years
have particularly incited the folk-imagination
to the creation of these weirdest legends in the
weirdest, most fantastic forms. The famine
of 1912 produced the black cow, the bull and
deer speaking with human voice. Still more
prolific was the last and most terrible famine
of 1921-22. One widespread tale, a prediction
of the coming horrors, crops up in various
places and guises. Here is a Siberian version
of it:

In the spring of this year a *mujik* was driving his empty wagon to Tuloon. On the way
he caught up with an old *baba* who cried out
from the roadside:

"Give me a lift, little uncle!"

"Don't you see," replied the *mujik*, "the horse is tired. Twenty versts we've gone already and it's heavy going."

"Anyhow," repeated the *baba*, "give me a lift. I'm light as a feather." So insistently did she beg that at last the *mujik* told her to climb on. They drove ahead, but in a short time the horse was panting, all covered with foam.

"Eh!" exclaimed the *mujik*, "you said you didn't weigh anything, but you're as heavy as a cow. The horse can hardly drag us."

"*Neechevo*," said the *baba*. "Just look over your left shoulder." The *mujik* looked and turned white with horror. All around lay droves of cattle, dead and dying.

"Now," said the *baba*, "take a look over your right shoulder." The *mujik* looked and saw great stacks of corn and wheat, but all drooping and without ears.

"And now glance upward," said the *baba*. So he did and there was a long black procession of people with coffins and lighted candles.

"Here I get off," said the *baba*. "Have a care. I warn you to say nothing to any one or I shall trample you to death." The *mujik* turned around and saw beneath the skirts of the *baba* not a woman's feet, but the hoofs of a cow. Thus, according to popular legend, was prophesied the widespread famine of 1921-22.

Hardest hit of all were the bread-bearing provinces of Saratov and Samara. Here all depends upon the caprices of the sky. Here is special significance to the peasant proverb, "It is not the earth that gives the harvest, but the sky." This year it flings down abundant rains, and the crops spring luxuriant from the rich black loam. Next year only sunshine, and the crops shrivel and vanish before the eyes. One may read the story of these dread dry years in the Old Chronicles (*Letopis*) preserved in the parish churches. Thus from Ivanovka on the Volga:

1880.—Blue skies all summer, the harvest was from two to six *poods* a *dessyatine*. Complaints about hunger more and more increase. Our answer to all those asking for the sake of Christ: "We ourselves are beggars."

1890.—A cloudless spring. The hunger-wounded, after four non-harvest years took heart, but from May 22, seventy days, not a drop of rain. Again despair.

"Blue sky. Cloudless blue sky." These are the fair words that always preface the story of crop disaster in the Volga Basin. So it was in the horror year of 1921. The blue skies of May and June turn brazen in July. Ninety rainless days. The crops burn to the roots. The cattle turn into bone-racks. The camel humps—reserve food—shrink to flapping bunches of skin. The granaries stand empty-bellied like the people. The last grain is blown from the cracks. The last bread, mixed with grass, sawdust, and horse-dung, is eaten. Despair seizes the villages. They sell their houses and horses for ten *poods*, five *poods*, even a few pounds of flour. Panic drives them into flight to Moscow, Siberia, the Ukraine. On top of

[129]

hunger, plague and typhus. No lights in the town. No wheeling flocks of pigeons. The stricken fall dead in the streets. Frozen corpses are corded in front of the hospital. The dead wagons cart them away to trenches.

One of those death wagons now brings me wood to Kvalinsk from the island, and I ask the driver to tell me about the famine.

"There is nothing to tell," he replies. "We ate our bread. When that was gone, we ate rats, cats, grass and weeds. When they were gone, we ate each other—then we died."

There, in brief, is the story of 1921. The living that one meets are survivers of a holocaust. All of them have a soul-shriving story of that hunger hell through which they passed —all these peasants thronging the bazaar to-day, shouting, trading, singing, scolding, offering their products to the passerby.

"Dear little doves! Sweet little swans! Stop and look!" cries a woman in a red *sarafan* and yellow *platok*, standing by a cow-drawn cart piled with potatoes. An old man fixes an appraising eye upon them and the little woman breaks out again more eloquently.

"Don't call them potatoes, little uncle. They're just sugar—only a ruble a sack."

"Come, come! Have you no God?" retorts the old man. "Fifty kopecks would be a robbery."

"What? Would I sin! That's for the young ones who have forgotten their Lord God, not for us, old ones, who smell of our coffins."

"Sixty kopecks!" says the old man crossing himself. "And God forgive you for asking a ruble for such a big food."

"A sin on my soul for stealing from my children!" declares the little woman. "But take them as a gift at eighty kopecks."

The old man carries them off at seventy kopecks—all of them. The money knotted in her handkerchief, the little woman munches a chunk of black bread, her eyes glistening eagerness.

"Tell me about the famine year, little aunt," say I.

"My white hairs will tell you," she answers, pushing back her yellow *platok* displaying a whitened head. "Before the famine they were brown as our wheat land.

"We were not rich, for the grain levy stripped us. But we had a camel and in 1920 we planted four *dessyatines* with bread.

"In November my *mujik*, coming back from the Volga, said there was a bad omen for next year's harvest—the ice had frozen smooth as a mirror. That's the sign the men believe in. But we women take our signs from the cattle after the winter when they are driven to pasture. That spring the pope said the prayers and sprinkled them, the cow-herd raised his whip. We shivered when we saw a red cow pushing ahead—if she went first it meant a fire. A white cow horned past her and we crossed ourselves for joy—for a white cow foretells a harvest. Then suddenly the red and white cows locked horns and as the cow-herd's whip cracked, three black cows plunged ahead, taking the lead as the herd broke for pasture.

" 'Virgin of Kazan! Save us from hunger!' I prayed. The Communists laugh at this. But what do they know, the Without Godders?

"Well, bread came up all green in April, then it stood still. It never grew high enough for a mouse to hide in. Six Sundays the rain prayers were said in the church. Six times we carried ikons round the fields. But no rain. The sins of the people were too great. Once Ilya's thunder chariot rumbled across the sky, but there was not rain enough to wet a calf.

"Thirty *poods* of seed we put in the earth— only six were born to be reaped. Ten *poods* we got from our cow and clothes that we sold. It wasn't so bad in the fall. For there were gophers that Shura caught in the meadows and there were crows. Misha got them by climbing trees at night, snatching them from their roost. Then there was a leg from the Tartar's horse that died; the hide we boiled in the *stchee* with nettles, the bones we ground into flour. We put everything into the bread—acorns and willow bark. At first the children cried, because

[133]

it was bitter. Then they cried, because there was so little of it.

"Then my *mujik* said, 'Bread won't come to the belly, the belly must go after bread.' So he and Shura went away with the camel that looked like a ghost. The peasants of Penza had never seen a camel. The Anti-Christ, they called it. With their ikons they came out and knelt before the camel, praying: 'O Little Mother of Smolensk! Carry it away from us! Let it go back to the evil on the Volga, only take it away from us!'

"But the poor camel died. My *mujik* died. Only Shura came back, bringing a sack of flour. If the children had had their way, they would have eaten the flour raw, eaten it in a day. When I went out I had to tie them up with a chain. Soon this bread was gone, but it was March and there were birds and swamp roots and green bark. 'We can eat anything, even oak-leaves like the camel!' Shura would say, trying to make the little ones laugh.

"They died before the relief kitchen opened, and now only Shura and I are left."

"And the new cow," I reminded her.

"Yes, and there's two hundred *poods* of potatoes this fall, and one hundred *poods* of wheat. God has forgiven our sins."

I turn into the *izvoschik* row and listen to the story of Inazarov, the Tartar.

"One morning, Tagir, my son, drove down by the mosque to sell a load of birch leaves. He didn't come back by night. I went up and down the bazaar a hundred times, there was no trace of him. Next day a peasant said he saw him driving off towards the big white church.

"I got the militia, and following tracks of Tagir's *lapti* in the snow, we came to the house of a man from the Eternal Khutor. We burst open the gate. The man swore he had never seen my son. But we found birch leaves in the courtyard. Then my horse's bridle. Then fresh horse meat salted away in barrels. Finally, we pried up the kitchen floor, and

[135]

there under the boards, was Tagir and another boy, their heads hammered in. 'Allah! Punish him!' I cried. Before the militia could stop me I nearly brained the *Shaitan* (devil), with a *duga*. They bound his hands and with a rope around his neck led him to the jail while we rushed on him and beat his back with knouts. Three days later he died, but the judge let me go. 'Any man would have done the same,' he said."

A few months later not only the horse, but the boys would have been salted away in barrels. To such desperation were people driven by starvation—to corpse-eating and cannibalism. Out of bushes human wolves sprang on the defenseless and killed them. Eight corpses were stolen at night from the morgue that Tsibushkin, the Mordvinian, was guarding. Fingers and ears were found in the meat jelly sold in the bazaar. The meat-pies at the wharf had unusual sweetness—human flesh. A taste for it developed. Brothers devoured sisters. Parents their children. Mothers the baby at their breast. Secret instructions came out of Moscow to be lenient with the flesh eaters. In the jail they were put in separate cells to keep them from tearing each other to pieces.

The triumph of Hunger over Man! Maddened by starvation, he sinks below the level of the beast.

But the record is not all grisly and ghastly. If the famine year showed the depths to which human spirit may fall, it showed likewise the heights to which it can rise. The triumph of Man over Hunger. Men starving themselves to death to save others from starving. Not only dying for family and children, but for society.

Walking over the hill with Obrosikhin, the Red Commander, I drew from him the story of his Bolshevik father, peasant of Brikovka village: "Night and day he worked on famine relief. When I came back from the North with flour I didn't know him. He filled the doorway, looking like a giant swelled up by hunger. Half of his grain he had given to the poor. His share of the bread I brought, he pretended to eat, but he gave that away too. I called him a fool; but he laughed. And he died laughing."

He did not die in vain. In his son, the Red Commander, and in his daughter—devoted servants of Communism—the Bolshevik father lives on.

In the same spirit was the story of the gray-*shubaed*, deep-eyed man crouched up on the wharf awaiting the night steamer.

"I was still in the cavalry at Kazan when news of the famine came. With eighty rubles collected by my comrades, I bought two bags of flour and hurried on to Buzuluk. Everything, everybody had a shrunken starving look. I didn't know my own home, no red geraniums in the windows, no straw on the roof. A strange, gaunt woman answered my knock.

" 'Come and sit down,' she said. But a sudden fear came over me, and I could not. I asked for my mother.

" 'Died on the way to Kazan for flour,' she replied.

" 'My father?' I questioned.

" 'Died of typhus.'

" 'My four brothers?' I named them each in turn. Three were dead from hunger. The youngest in the hospital. I covered my face with my hands and said, 'I will sit down while you tell me again, that I may believe what you say is true.'

"I got up and went up to find my brother. I found him dead. His head was swollen like a tub. In his mouth was still the grass he had been chewing. I ran out on the street, ran into an old woman, knocking her down. One bag of flour was still in my arms, I threw it at her and ran on and on into the face of a storm. The snow was blinding me, a fire within was burning me and I fell.

"I woke up in a typhus barrack. From a skeleton on the next cot I learned how my eldest brother had died. He was a Communist in charge of an American Relief Kitchen. The food was rationed out for children only. Those were his orders, and that was the way he carried them out. He died of starvation. A week later came the order to ration the staff-workers as well—but it came a week too late!"

"You too are a Communist?" I asked.

"Yes, the world needs happiness."

"And your job now?"

"I'm an agronomist. The world needs bread."

IV

"The world needs bread!"

Well, the world has bread. The Volga Basin is full of it. Nature has relented. Bread once more in the bread basket of the world. These fields burned bare in the famine of 1921, and the half-famine of 1924, are staggering with the biggest harvest in decades.

Bread! Bread! Bread!

It pours down from the hills in long files of creaking wagons, and in camel caravans out of the steppe under the harvest moon. It pours into cavernous maws of the big elevators along the river front, into the roaring mills grinding away night and day. It pours life into the veins of the Russian state, loosing the tides of trade and commerce. It puts shining new shoes and dresses upon the girls. It sets forges glowing and anvils ringing in the blacksmith shops. It calls the pigeons back from the dead and sets them in blue flocks wheeling above the bazaar. It brings up deep welling songs from the new recruits rolling in from the villages. It puts laughter and hope into the masses of peasants crowding into the autumn fair.

This year it is a Harvest Festival. A Carnival of Bread. For it the bakers have turned out tens of thousands of loaves. They are stacked up all over the place.

Bread in bags! waiting to be carried on steamers.

Bread in cords! ready to be loaded into wagons for the workers on the new irrigation dam across the Volga.

Bread on legs! long files of it, marching into

the Tartar Children's Home. That's the way
it seems, so enormous are the loaves borne on
the heads of the little laughing Tartar boys.
The beggars' sacks are crammed with bread,
and the bazaar dog, that goes from stall to
stall standing on his hind legs a-begging, has
grown so fat, he wobbles. An Epicurean now,
he wrinkles his nose at the black bread—white
bread, or none at all.

As for the peasants, there is no holding them
in. The harvest has gone to their heads, and
with the help of vodka, all peasant caution and
concealment are thrown to the winds. To-day
no lamentations about taxes, high prices on
city products, low prices on village products.
To-day the peasants are boasting.

"I tell you, Victor Mikhilovitch, one hundred and fifty *poods* from every *dessyatine*."

"Believe me or not, Ivan Petrovitch, I got
two hundred. I don't know where to store it."

This is solemn truth. The teacher Matvey
of Yershovka tells me, if there were no debts
and taxes to pay, his wheat would suffice for

twenty years; from this one harvest the village could eat white bread for seven years.

In the samovar tent by the grain *kiosk* the peasants, packed three deep around the tables, are in deliriums of delight.

"Hey, there, American!" they cry, beckoning me with vodka bottles. "Come in and drink a toast to the harvest and Little Mother Earth."

"Two more years like this and we can dam up the Volga with it, we'll build a wheat mountain to the moon," says Red Beard Borodin of Popovka.

"*Yeh Bogoo!* We'll flood up Europe with it," exclaims another. "American wheat has had its way too long in the streets of Europe. Now Volga wheat is coming on and boost him off the sidewalk. Like this!" He made a long lunging kick. I made as if to write this down in my note-book.

"No! No!" interrupted Peter Ivanovich. "American Wheat was good to us in the famine year. He saved our lives. Put it down this way: When American Wheat meets Volga Wheat in Europe, he will take his cap off and say, 'Oh, good morning, Volga Wheat! So you are here also. My high respects to you!' Like this!" He made a low sweeping bow.

Laughter. Another samovar. More vodka. The clapping of hands marking the clinching of bargains in the cattle market. Songs from the *mogarich* drinkers out of the tavern windows. Clatter of hammers and boards on new buildings going up. Crowds of buyers, ten rows deep, at the all-coöperative counters. The rumble of tractors taking the hill back of the town.

And this is Kvalinsk, the *volost* hardest hit by the famine on all the right bank of the Volga; and across the river is Pugachev, in all Russia no district so famine-scourged.

Traveling along the highroads, one still finds marks of that famine: Here the white trunk of willow peeled of its bark for food. There a nailed-up house whose owner never returned from his long pilgrimage after bread.

A coughing *mujik* with the city disease—tuberculosis—off to the peasant palace in Livadia. Deepest of all the famine mark on the budget —a third of all *volost* expenditures going to the five orphan-houses.

But all these scars are healing. Healing fast. Deep and fertile is the black Volga soil. Deep and mighty the virility of the Russian peasant. Tremendous the recuperative forces of the Soviet lands.

VI
THE BOLSHEVIST BOY SCOUTS

VI

THE BOLSHEVIST BOY SCOUTS

It was a gala day when I visited the Dikanka school. There was an exhibition of embroidery—cross-stitch towels by the boys, dresses by the girls. There was chorus singing of "Beyond the Stone Mountains," "In the Meadows by the Birch Trees." Then a chant of the Revolution with the words: "Holy army of labor."

"Stop!" cried Natalie Alexandrovna. "In-

stead of 'holy' it should be 'battling.'" And
so they sang it. The children liked best the
song that closed each verse with a shout of
Slava! Slava! Glory! Glory! Followed
the "Hopak" and "Snowstorm," danced to the
thrumming of the balalaikas. Then out in the
yard for a game of cat-and-mouse. The new
Volost President and I took our turns, racing in
and out of the wide circle, until at last the big
American mouse fell into the paws of the little
Ukrainian cat, to the shrieking joy of the children, and we were friends for life.

Next day I was merrily shaking hands with
all my friends, until in one hand I met a sharp
rebuff. It shot straight above the boy's head,
and was rigidly held there, as he said: "With
Young Leninists hand-shaking is abolished.
It wastes time; it spreads disease."

Thus I met Panas, my first Young Leninist,
or Pioneer, and next night was guided by him
to their quarters in an old house beyond the
church. To our knock on the door came a
challenge:

"Who goes there? Friend of the workers and peasants—or enemy?"

"Friends! Let us enter!"

There was a scuffle of feet, voices mumbling, "I've lost the key!" "Oh, you ninny!" Then the door opened into a room dimly lit by a smoking lamp and a candle. On the walls were immense portraits of Lenin and the poet Schevchenko and, in big Ukrainian letters, the "Laws of the Pioneers."

A pioneer is true to the business of the working class, and to the biddings of Ilyich.

A Pioneer is younger brother to the *Komsomols* and Communists.

A Pioneer does not smoke, drink or swear.

A Pioneer is kind to useful animals—against grasshoppers, mice and prairie dogs he wages a merciless fight.

A Pioneer studies hard. He who does not love books is no Pioneer at all.

A Pioneer sits, stands and walks not bending over. Otherwise he will look like a bent, broken old man, and his heart will not work rightly.

[151]

A Pioneer washes himself carefully, not forgetting his neck and ears. Remembering the teeth are friends of the stomach, he cleans them daily.

There were five more similar injunctions. They are not the standard Pioneer Laws, but a special version made by Ladyr, the leader, or *Vojak* as he is called. He was a stocky, swarthy, benign lad of sixteen, lost in an enormous overcoat inherited from a soldier and altered only by cutting off the sleeves at the elbows. His father was killed by the Whites, and he lived with his mother in a house which I might find by "going down the East Lane till you see a lopsided hut with a lopsided goat inside a lopsided fence—that's where we live!" There were no marks of poverty on his wit or imagination.

He led us to a seat behind a table, facing about sixty children, and the interrupted debate on washing the floors for the October holidays was resumed. In the boys' opinion that had "always been a woman's job."

"Yes," says *Vojak* Ladyr. "But it will not always be. The boys must not dodge the hard and dirty jobs. If they do they are not Pioneers."

Ten-year-old Luzenko takes up the cudgel for the girls. He holds that Pioneers should not be divided into boys and girls, but into the big and the little. The former should wash the floors, the latter gather leaves and weave garlands. So it was voted, and the club took up cases of discipline.

"Marfa Lisovik, you have been absent twice. What for?"

She hesitates, and finally blurts out: "I was afraid of the dark."

"Huh!" snorts Ladyr. "In foreign lands they put Pioneers in prisons and torture them, and our Pioneer is afraid of the dark!"

Marfa protests that prison has no terrors for her, but each night when she was about to set out for the club, *babushka* told her tales of Baba Yaga, so terrible that when she opened the door it put a shiver in her back. Cunning old *babushka!* Less resourceful, it seems, were other *babas* in keeping their children away from the club. The usual device was to take them to church. Such was the excuse given by two Pioneers. This provokes the *Vojak* to a lengthy discourse on religion. I learn that as long as children are economically dependent on parents, they must obey. If commanded to go to church, the Pioneer must go, but he should strive not to pray or cross himself, and, if possible, not light a candle before an ikon. In the same spirit, at weddings or christenings, if a Pioneer is offered a glass of *samogon* by his father, he may take it, but must strive not to drink it, but to pour it on the floor or out of the window.

It is evident that to *Vojak* Ladyr parents are thorns in the flesh. But he accepts them philosophically. None of the usual flippancy of youth in his treatment of them. Carefully he explains to the Pioneers how the elder generation have grown up in religion and drink and private property; that they are not to be

blamed for their bad ideas, habits and prejudices, but to be treated with kindly tact.
Humor them, don't antagonize them.

Not in vain his teachings, the fruit of it most
apparent in my first Pioneer, Panas. To my
question why hand-shaking was abolished, he
explains that two hundred thousand Russians
had died of typhus, twenty thousand of whom
must have gotten the germs by shaking hands.

I point out that, while in the papers there
was a campaign against hand-shaking, and in
Soviet offices there are signs against it, it goes
on just the same, even amongst Communists
and *Komsomols*.

"Yes," he replies. "But one must be patient
with the elder generation. They won't change
very much. They can't be cured. It is for
Young Leninists to show the way." Critical
but tolerant.

Follows now the administration of the oath
to a new Pioneer. The *Vojak* has none of the
paraphernalia of the city Pioneers—no whistle
or drums, or red kerchiefs—only the salute, the

five fingers of the right hand close clasped together, raised above the head. The fingers are the five continents where there are oppressed, for whose freedom fights the Pioneer. Held above the head to show that their interests are higher than all.

The candidate now repeats the oath: "I give my promise and strengthen it with my solemn word that I will be true to the toilers, will toil hard myself, follow the commandments of Ilyich, the laws and customs of the Pioneers."

"You are now a Pioneer in the Union of Socialist Soviet Republics. In the fight for the toilers be ready!" declares the *Vojak* impressively.

"Always ready!" replies the boy. Hard for a bashful boy to be so long the focus of all eyes. In the happy relief from the strain he shoves his hands into his pockets.

"He violates Law Eight!" pipes up a boy. The *Vojak* confirms the young constitutionalist, quoting: "A Pioneer putting his hands into his pockets is not *always ready.*"

Now the Political Lottery. Orator Luzenko and another favorite are elected judges, and take their places on the bench beside the *Vojak*. Five pencil stubs are produced, and go scribbling on paper held on walls, knees and neighbors' backs. The slips are rolled, put into a hat and shaken up. Each Pioneer in turn draws one out.

"Well, let's see what question you've got?" says the *Vojak* to the boy in the front row, and taking the slip he reads:

"What did the October Revolution give the people?"

"Land, factories and freedom," comes the glib response.

"What is Communism?"

"A society where there will be no war, no rich and poor, but all free toilers," just as glibly.

"What class does a Pioneer never help?"

"Those who exploit the toil of others—rich, bandits and *nepmen*."

These are easy questions, studied in the club

over and over again. Nearly every Pioneer knows the answers to them by heart.

"Who was Comrade Lib—nit?" mumbles a girl reading her own slip.

"Liebknecht," corrects Ladyr, "who was he?"

"I don't know," falters the girl.

"Judges, judges! Write her down!" cry several voices with satisfaction, and the judges solemnly reply, "She is written!" Another gets written down because he confuses Bakunin and Bucharin. The questions: "Whom should one obey—father or mother?" "Which is better —an ox or a horse?" are ruled out as non-political. Other questions: "Where was Schevchenko born?" "Who was Kerensky?" And finally, taking a slip from a little girl, the *Vojak* reads, "Who is Ladyr?"

Great joy, the audience breaking into wild peals of childish laughter, when the little girl stammers:

"Why, it's you!"

More joy when Judge Magas, himself unable to tell when Lenin was born, has to write himself down. Merriest of all when the *Vojak* attempts to tell "What is specialization?" One way, then another, he wrestles with it, and finally gives it up, saying it is in his head all right, but he can't explain it. The merciless judges write him down.

At last the questions are finished. The names of the "written down" are read and the offenders are summoned before the High Court of the Political Lottery. "Pioneer Kalnik!" says Judge Panas sternly. "You didn't know the answer, you must therefore recite a verse."

"No, no!" cry several voices. "Make him sing!"

"Pioneers!" interrupts Ladyr. "You chose the judges. Let them determine the punishments."

The culprit recites a verse from Schevchenko. "Pioneer Drooshko, a riddle! What is it that has no eyes, but shows the way to others— has no brains, but knows how to count?"

"It is the sign-post marking the versts."

"Next riddle! What has forty coats—none of them ever buttoned?"

"A cabbage!"

Another defaulter dances the "Hopak." Then the judges make up a chorus of several of the "written down." Among their songs is a ditty of the New Year masqueraders, full of dire threats to houses which do not give them gifts.

> If you do not give me eggs,
> I will break your chickens' legs!

The *Vojak* protests that these words violate Law Four. Pioneers should be kind to animals and not break their legs. Moreover the chickens might belong to a poor peasant, and even if they belonged to a *kulak*, Pioneers must never proceed by acts of individual violence.

On the whole, the *Vojak* is well satisfied with the Political Lottery. Another night it goes wrong, and he orders a trial. For judges, five children are chosen. The defender is young orator Luzenko. Ladyr himself is prosecutor. He begins:

"We need discipline, Comrade Pioneers! Some members act as if they were not in a club, but a bazaar, and go chattering like *babas* at a village well. Then there are irrelevant questions. For instance, 'Who were the gladiators?' Probably the author of this has just read a book about them and wants to make boast of it. Before such a question is given it should be studied. The worst social criminals are the prompters. They often prompt the wrong answers. I ask the judges to rule that every prompter and every one prompted be excluded from the club for two nights. That their names be written down on the blackboard and, for three offenses, declared members of the Counter-Revolution and excluded altogether."

The defender makes no attempt to ward off the prosecutor's attack on Pioneers' discipline and the character of questions. He declares that "His accusations against promptings are unfundamental. Let him say who were prompters and who were prompted. Besides, if a Pioneer knows the answer, it is hard not to whisper it, and the Pioneer who doesn't know the answer will know if he is prompted a little. The demands of the prosecutor are too hard, and I ask the judges to refuse them."

"Judges!" shouts the prosecutor, "the defender doesn't know the first principles of Communism. I tell you prompting is never right. No one ever prompted Lenin, and no one who follows him will depend on somebody else's brains—but on his own. My demands are just and I confirm them!"

The trial closes with the *Vojak* in great indignation. The judges go out into the corridor to confer. In a half-hour they return with the verdict:

"In order that the work shall pass more organizedly the High Court of the Political Lottery declares that: (1) Pioneers must behave themselves more in conformity with the principles of Communism. (2) Questions must be based only on the subjects studied. Songs, verses and riddles must be learned in advance. (3) Prompters and prompted shall be declared renegade Pioneers in the Union of Socialist Soviet Republics and before the working class of the whole world."

VII
COMRADE COUNT MEDEM SEES IT THROUGH

VII

COMRADE COUNT MEDEM SEES IT THROUGH

Dusk in the old *volost* town of Khvalynsk. An autumn wind howls round the red tribunal that looms from the square. A bent figure with a flickering lantern and tray huddles up by a black wall, waiting. This is Klukhin, eighteen years the Mayor of Kvalinsk, now a hawker of cigarettes.

"Good evening, Michael Ivanovich," says a man coming up with a sack of potatoes on his back.

"My respects to you, Count," says the ex-mayor, starting up. "What will you have?"

"A package of *makhorka*," says the sack-carrier, fumbling ten kopecks out of his pocket.

So I first met Alexander Ottovich Medem, one-time Marshal of Nobility, Count in his own right, his father Governor of Old Novgorod, his lineage going back to the Baltic barons and Peter the Great.

The Medem estate lies near the Waterless Village, on the high bluffs of the Volga. A little lower, the under-cutting current, in 1902, washed down two hundred cottages. Had the Count's manor house stood on the bluffs it would have gone down with them. It stands safely back from the Volga on a treeless plain set in an oasis of springs and willows, white-edged against the black soil by a palisade of birches.

Back of it a massive red brick pile looms against the horizon like a cathedral—the Count's distillery, that produced one hundred thousand *vedros* of alcohol a year. On either side, long, low, black sheds stabling eight hundred cows, oxen and horses. To the east, the crosses of the Orthodox villages, furnishing the estate its muscles and sinews. To the north, the crescents of the Moslem villages, in harvest time moving out *en masse* with dogs, goats and children, turning the estate into a Tartar *stan*. More than a thousand Mussulmen, in the morning, making their prayers toward Mecca, and at night setting the plain blazing with their camp fires.

"What kind of landlord was the Count?" I asked an old *mujik* of Waterless Village.

"A good man," he replied, "always helping others. One rainy day, the wagon of a poor Tartar stuck in the mud. The Count, driving up in his *troika*, saw that the bony hack of a horse couldn't pull it out. He unharnessed one of his own and gave it to the poor fellow. Gave it to him outright. He was always doing this." This tale, in varying versions, I was to hear a hundred times. Now it is a Mordvinian that gets a horse free. Now a Chuvash. Now a Russian. A mania for giving away his horses, it seems, possessed the Count. If all the tales were true, how did he have any horses left? I went to the Count for the truth about the matter.

"Yes," he vaguely recalled, "I think my father once did give a horse to a Tartar."

That horse has grown now into hundreds, and continues to grow. The legend of the horse-giving Medem promising to take its place alongside of Stenka Razin. It suits the peasants. In dramatic form, it puts their approval on the Count and the conduct of his affairs. Not that they grow lyric about the golden past. On the contrary, they still sing songs about the black and bitter days toiling on the Count's estate.

They were sung for me by two Blagodatno peasants, Andrey Shookhin and Koozma Oreshkin, with long-drawn-out, wailing refrains. Finishing, they remarked: "But it was easier with him than with the other landlords." They told of being driven from Easter merrymaking out to the plowing, and of the horse whose teeth grabbed them by their hair and held them while they were knouted. Then they added: "But the Count was not to blame. It was the devil overseers, our own brothers, who did it."

The Count, like the Tsar, was able to deflect the people's anger on his subordinates. Peasants no longer say the Tsar was a good man. That belief is utterly and irrevocably dead. But they do say the Count was a good man. One hears it on every side. Of course, "good" is a term of relativity. It is the shining contrast of the Count against the dark background of other landlords that wins for him the ascription of "good," the favor and esteem of the peasants.

He was not high-handed, like his neighbors the Davidovs, putting a ruble fine on every chicken that flew on to his grounds. He didn't flaunt his wealth, like Shekhovalov, but in the fodder famine gave his horses the same ration as the peasant horses. He didn't rack-rent his tenants, like Tschukin, but let out his land at moderate sums. He didn't signalize his homecoming, like Vorontzov Dashkova, with a fanfare of trumpets and bells, riding down a lantern-strewn way through lines of kneeling villagers. He wasn't a waster, like Korsakov, hanging over the American Bar in Paris, chasing butterflies along the Riviera. He didn't sell his estate, like Prince Golitzin, and move to the city.

He lived with the peasants. He helped the burned-out find logs for new houses. He helped the Tartars steal their brides, loaning them horses. He worked out a plow best suited to the local soil and sold it at cost—twenty-one rubles. He wasn't afraid to drive a furrow, crack the whip over the oxen or lend a hand pulling a horse out of the Volga. He once carried a sick pony home on his back. He was a working count, like the great Count of Tula, who pointed his preachments about the dignity of labor by laboring himself.

An observation by the side. Count Tolstoy may have actually plowed more ground than Count Medem. Yet in the week that I was in

Yasnaya Polyana, I heard from no peasant the unqualified praise of Tolstoy that almost every peasant gives to Medem. Maybe, to the Tolstoy peasants, the acts of their Count had a smack of theatricalism—too moralistic and romantic.

Count Medem had more of the smell of earth on him, more reality in his work, and, unlike Tolstoy, he was able to communicate the spirit of it to his family. His sister, Maria Ottovna, was a doctor to the women. The Countess nursed many through the cholera epidemic. In the pleasant idyllism pictured by Turgenev in "Gentlefolks' Nests," the years rolled by, until comes that fateful year in the history of the Russian people—the summer of 1917.

The Count is roused one morning by a loud clatter in his courtyard. He looks out to see it filled with wagons—hundreds of them. He dresses hurriedly and goes out to the balcony.

"Good morning, *mujiks*, brothers. What did you come for?"

"Our wheat, our rye, our millet!" comes the

answer, laughing. The keys are brought out, the door unlocked, the granaries are emptied.

"Now the grain underground!" Always the Count believed the hiding place of these reserves was a secret. But the peasants know all. The grain goes. Then the horses and oxen. Then the land. They divided, plowed it, harrowed it and sowed it. "Just as we had done for the Count, we did now for ourselves. The land was ours now. All of it ours," exclaimed the old peasant rapturously, telling me the story of the seizure of the estate.

"And yet you will say he was a good landlord," I interjected.

"No!" he replied. "There is no such thing as a good landlord. He was a good man. But the land was never his, no more than the winds that blow over it or the Volga water that flow by it."

Let the Count show Nicholas the First's grant to his ancestors. Let him show the great seals on his own deed of inheritance. What of them? To the peasant, right to the soil is not vested in papers and titles but in one's hands, in one's ability to till, in one's self. When these hands cannot do it, their right to it is gone. It passes automatically into the hands that can. That's what it was doing on this fair morning in the summer of 1917.

These peasants clamoring into the courtyard had no feeling of being engaged in an act of spoliation. It was an act of restoration, an act of liberalism, the deliberate transfer of the land into the hands of its legitimate owners. Against Comrade Count Medem—as they now call him—there was no animosity. They gave him his share of the soil, tools and horses, and left him undisturbed in his manor house, and there were no excesses.

"If only Russia had had good landlords!" exclaim those who imagine that that might have staved off the Revolution. But could any one be more abounding in good works than the good Count of the Volga? Yet, though they had been a hundredfold greater, they couldn't have saved his land. But they did save his life.

And considering the fierce passions engendered by the Revolution, which put most counts in the graveyard or to flight into foreign lands, this is not a trifle. And be it said that these peasants were as resolutely insistent on the Count's right to life as to their own right to the land.

When a band of *Frontovics* landed at Waterless Village, declaring "Death to all *pometschiks!*" the peasants put in the proviso—"except Medem!" When the bandits were loose in the forest, six old peasants galloped beside him as a bodyguard through versts of winter storm. When the Count was lying in the Cheka prison, condemned to death, they drew up a big petition for his release. When the 1921 famine tightened its grip on the Volga basin, out of their scanty stores they brought him flour and products—and continued to do so. When at last he was ejected from the manor house, they loaded up their wagons with furniture and brought them to him in town.

And here in Khvalynsk he lives, a debonair

figure in his shining high boots and blue velvet Tartar hat, edged with sable. Not a tinge of gray in his bushy beard. A man without a worry, one would imagine—not a man with a household of seven, one an embecile for eighteen years, dressed, fed and put to bed like a baby. A man of leisure, one might imagine, spending his time traveling from resort to resort instead of from jail to jail. Nine times he was arrested; thrice sentenced to be shot.

It is said that a man is equal to any disaster, provided it is great enough. Count Medem is a striking example of this. Certainly he can't complain about the dimensions of his misfortune or his fall. From a palace to a three-room house. From a drove of eight hundred horses and cattle, to one cow and five chickens. From Marshal of the Nobility, to a commoner without a vote. From a man of wealth to a waterdrawer. Sometimes ninety buckets a day to carry. "I have a thirsty garden," he says with a smile.

"It's his religion that sustains him," his

friends assert. The Count is, indeed, a strict keeper of the fasts; candle in hand, he kneels for hours in the monastic church; he likes, like Dostoyevsky, to contemplate the peasants as the "God bearers." Not less devout are others of the old nobility, but sour and gloomy; one avoids them like a plague.

The Count, however, always sparkles with jests and laughter. He laughs at everything. The soldiers shooting the eyes out of a portrait of Alexander III and using it as a prop for a potato bin; the peasants knowing the secret of his underground stores; the Tartar cutting up one of his racing horses for meat; the old *mujik* lugging off the stone lions to grace his cattle-shed. He laughs at himself; burying in his garden the golden snuff-box, a gift to his ancestors from Catherine the Great, and never able to find it again; entrusting his silver plate to an officer's wife, who later married a Chekist; taking orders from those to whom he once gave orders; plodding on foot when he once rode in a *troika*.

"Why shouldn't one laugh? What can one do about it? So it was predestined, so it must be!"

With such happy fatalism he met the disasters of the Revolution. His friends in town professed this philosophy, and regaled him with it after the summer storm of 1917 had struck him and stripped him.

"Why, Count, it is inevitable. It's the Revolution!" they said, shrugging their shoulders, thinly veiling their bourgeois satisfaction in the downfall of a noble.

The Count bided his time. It came in the autumn, when this self-same bourgeoisie, bowled over by the blasts of October, crept whimpering to him for consolation. His turn to be calmly philosophic. "It's inevitable," he repeated, with a lift of the eyebrows. "It's the Revolution. It's all you wanted. Don't you remember how happy you were when the Tsar fell, Pavel Nikolaevitch? And, by the way, where is that nice red flag you were waving then? And you! Ivan Petrovich! how about

'Revolution Bringing New Life to Old Russia?' Lovely article that!"

With sardonic glee he watched the Revolution go down the social scale, until into the villages whistled the winter winds of 1918-20, laying tribute on the rich peasants, stripping the grain away from the very ones who had first stripped him. To all their sorrowing and raging his jocular reply: "Why, brothers, it's the Revolution. So it was predestined—so it needs must be."

There was no restraining the Count's humor and wit and satire. He carried them into his ordeals of trials and cross-questionings. Quite likely they helped carry him through. One night he took his last horse out of hiding to exercise on the Volga ice. A Commissar spied him. The Count spied the Commissar and at once sent the horse to his White Guard brother hiding in a Tartar village. At headquarters next morning, the Commissar asked:

"Where is your horse?"

"With my brother," the Count replied.

"And where is your brother?"

"With my horse."

"Come, now, be serious!" said the Commissar.

"I am serious," replied the Count. "I don't want to lose my horse or my brother."

Again, a servant, in revenge for his interference with her amours, reported a revolver hidden in the Count's piano. He returned to find a searching squad in his room.

"Very serious, Count, we have found a weapon."

"How could you help finding it when you knew where it was?"

"You know it is against Proletarian Law to conceal weapons?"

"Quite true!" he replied, "but for counts it makes an exception." Luckily, he could produce a revolver-permit signed by a previous Commissar.

But even at the risk of his neck he would indulge his humor. Most of the Bolshevik captors, it seems, appreciated a White who came before them—not cringing or whining—but with laughter and repartee. But he was suspect, and always they were on his trail.

"They must have liked my company," says the Count. "Always they were inviting me to come and sit with them."

Arrests, protocols, inquisitions without number. What does it show? The diabolical effort of the Bolsheviks to trap an innocent man at all costs, as the Whites would say? Or shall it be written down as a singular example of their infinite patience amidst perils and perplexities, their determination not to do injustice? A Counter-Revolutionist at heart. Why didn't they kill him and be done with it?

The Count often wonders at it himself. "But so it was predestined to be." Fate gave him his life and he makes the most of it.

He still has the Volga. The view from the high bluffs across the steppe, the Count declares, is unequaled in the world. When his friends urge him to come to crowded Moscow, he exclaims: "Leave the Volga to live in a rabbit warren! Never!"

Then there are his books—French, English, German, a thousand volumes. True, not on his own shelves, but in the public library. But they are his to browse in, and now he has time to indulge to the full his literary and historical tastes.

There are his five daughters and nieces. Two of them are choir singers, the eldest a teacher of French and English, at a hundred rubles a month. Their accomplishments are no longer the decorations of gentlewomen, they have been turned to the service of society and the winning of bread.

Nor has the Count lost interest in his old estate. Now it is a *Sovkhoz*, a Soviet Farm. These model farms are generally held by the peasants in high contempt. "Very useful to us they are," they remark sarcastically, "they show us how to conduct our farming." *Sovkhoz* Number 68 is a shining exception. The fields, once plowed by the Count's two hundred oxen, are now turned by ten chugging tractors. The white brick edifice, that once housed the Count's family, now houses twelve labor families and a village school. It is piped and steam-heated, fuel furnished by the straw that formerly was thrown away. And it shows a profit, thanks to the Communist managers. One of them, Pugachev, former lackey of the Count, occasionally spends a night in town talking with his former master about seeds, soil and drainage on the old estate.

The Count often contradicts himself. Now the old Black Hundred has the upper hand, now the modernist. He will declare that all Communists are scoundrels or blockheads, then sit up till morning with them, arguing agriculture and religion. He will quote Dostoyevsky as prophesying that Russia will pass into the hands of the Jews, then swear fidelity to the one Jew in the town. He will lament the passing of the great statesmen of Russia, then read with admiration the speeches of the Soviet leaders, and chortle over the diplomatic thrusts of Chicherin.

On one point, however, there is never wavering or doubt—the ultimate destiny of Russia and its place in the world. While bourgeoisie fall on their knees before the cultures, civilizations and governments of the West—not the Count. He views them with the cynicism of an old Slavophil. Bringing back my London papers and New York magazines, he exclaims: "What are they coming to in Europe and America? Madhouses! Idiots! What they need is a Revolution!"

VIII
VILLAGE JUSTICE

VIII

VILLAGE JUSTICE

I

FIFTEEN cases for the People's Court have piled up in the back villages of Khvalynsk Volost. That means a hundred peasants, each making a twenty- or thirty-verst journey down from the hills to Khvalynsk.

"Instead of coming to you, we are asking the Court to come to us." This is the request that Red-beard Lopukhov from Pine Tar Village delivers to Judge Khonin.

[189]

"But the Court has no funds for travel," explains the Judge.

"If you will come, we will furnish horses, food, lodging," says the emissary.

"Agreed," replies the Judge.

A bitter cold December day when the *yemshik* drew up before our doors. I fitted myself into the prosecutor's felt boots (*valenki*), the prosecutor into the Judge's; the Judge confiscated his boy's. Loading ourselves into a twig basket resembling a bathtub on runners, we climbed up the gully road. A long drive buffeting the wind on the high plateau above the Volga, and at last Pine Tar Village and into a big wall-on-wall fight proceeding in honor of the first fall of snow.

Pine Tar is a big village—six hundred and fifty houses, and a center for many near-by hamlets.

A well-to-do village. Drawing a double income by adding to its grain fields great onion beds irrigated by many springs.

A cunning village. "Six hundred *dessyatines*

sowed" were the returns officially made to the tax appraiser. Hail beat down the crops, and claims were put in for twelve hundred *dessyatines* damaged.

A stubborn village. Sixty thousand *poods* was the grain requisition levied on it in 1919. The village heads announced, "Thirty thousand is all that we will give." Commissars came, arrested the village heads, sent them off to Khvalynsk. A new assembly was called, new heads elected, but the same reply: "Thirty thousand we will give, and not one *pood* more." They in turn were arrested and a Red division billeted in the village. The peasants hid their grain in the earth, sold it to Tartars in the night, carried it off in boots and aprons, distilled it into *samogon;* anything but give it up to the threatening Commissars, who, after a year's effort, gathered in but fifteen thousand *poods*—half what the village agreed to give.

An Old Believers' village. Founded by the Sharpshooters (*streltzi*) exiled thither after the revolt against Peter the Great, and enduring

century-long persecution from the Orthodox
State Church. Their bells were silenced; even
the repairing of their prayer house was forbidden; and by special order of the Tsar sentinels were placed at the doors to bar all entrance.

Now the bells swing free, and their soft
chiming at evening dusk led me to the prayer
house.

Opening the door, I stepped into the Middle
Ages—into a big-bearded, black-caftaned peasant mass, white-framed by long rows of *platok*-
headed women. In the center an enormous
book was held aloft in many upstretched arms,
the strange Slavonic script lit by a gigantic
green candle, while out of the painted pages
forty peasants chanted the ancient liturgy, calling, with incredible rapidity, "God's mercy on
us!" surely not less than a thousand times.
Even the Judge, who holds a Tolstoyan animus
against the Church, but whom I induced to look
in, admitted it was weirdly impressive.

Jeweled ikons, white incense clouds, golden-
clad priests swaying with the censers, wor-

shipers in deep prostrations to the floor, endless signing of the cross in unison, hundreds of candle flames pin-pricking the dark, and somber, big-eyed saints gazing down from their silver frames. I might have succumbed to the mesmerism of the ceremony were it not for profane thoughts about the combustibility of those long beards waving so freely among the candles. Were virgin beards somehow fireproof? Or do they sometimes burn up? For Old Believers this would be a twofold tragedy: the loss of decoration in this world and of a passport into the next.

With these prophet-bearded men in great flowing coats the village looks as though it had stepped out of the Old Testament. And the resemblance is not merely superficial.

II

It was with the old patriarchal family, the Agaphonovs, that the Court was lodged. Four generations inhabiting two rooms, and on top of them came we—six in number. Samovar and soup were set up by *babushka*, and out of the Judge's sausage roll, the prosecutor's apples, and the defender's meat, we made a communal feast. After the roster of the morrow's cases, crimes of the village were called for. The Soviet jurists were young, but they already had a professional taste for crime, like doctors for disease. All that evening we heard the crimes of Pine Tar Village, past, present, and prospective.

They began with the story of what had happened at this very table around which we sat. Here, one saint's day, sat two big *mujiks*, Vassily Nazarovich and Yegor Luda, celebrating their lifelong friendship in demijohns of vodka. They sang the old songs together, kissed, embraced, calling each other "Little red sun," "Blue dove," "Little white dove"—all the Russian terms of endearment. But all so inadequate to the exaltation of their feelings! Nothing left but that peculiar means by which the peasant expresses the extremes of his affection—the fists.

[194]

"For love's sake, Vassily," said Yegor, "let's go out and fight!"

The two giants, squaring off, rushed at each other like bulls, voices crying, bodies crushing, fists thudding, crimsoning the snow with blood. Finally a sledge-hammer blow on Yegor's temple, knocking him dead.

Vassily, grief-stricken, wanted to kill himself. But so obviously it was "a fight for love's sake" that Vassily's sentence was nominal—three months' jail and the injunction never to fight again.

The greatest tragedy in the village annals was in the blizzard of 1912, on a howling night that muffled every sound. It happened in the *izba* next door. Zakhar, a sober, God-fearing, industrious *mujik*, suddenly picked up the usual instrument of peasant execution, an ax, and proceeded to chop his family to pieces. The six-year-old son desperately rushed the father, but was shoved out of doors, and beat his way through the storm to the Agaphonovs. When Jacob pushed his way into the house he found blood spurts on the ceiling, the daughter headless, the wife in shreds, and Zakhar on top of the stove, smoking.

The murder has passed into poetry, a long epic ballad that was half sung, half recited by son Jacob in a steady monotone. Under its influence Grandfather Ivan, on top of his stove, drifted off to sleep.

Time for all to turn in. The last baby was put in a springing cradle hung from the ceiling. Father Anton and his wife lay on the bed. Son Jacob and wife stretched out on the floor. Likewise grandson Feodor and tangles of children. Likewise the Court. Removing coats, we stretched out in a row, trying to sleep in the equatorial heat engendered by this mass of humanity and two mammoth stoves. Too much for me. I went out to the cow shed. Later, judge and prosecutor came out to bunk with me in the straw, to brush away the snow that sifted through the cracks, and to speculate upon the ferocious passions that lie latent in these mild, blue-eyed, apostle-faced peasants.

III

In the morning we found the hall for the court filled with smoke and fumes from a leaking stove. "Impossible!" said the Judge. The schoolhouse was proposed—that meant turning out the children. "Impossible!" said the Judge. Some one said, "Why not open the windows?" Attention, skeptics about the advance of revolutionary ideas among the masses! In a Russian village in winter time the windows were opened! As the smoke and fumes went out the crowd came in, and straightway the hall was warming up with a thousand oxygen-burning lungs.

"Before court opens, let's have a meeting," said the Judge. The theory of Soviet law and legislation was the subject of the Judge's discourse. It was formal, heavy with verbiage. Deeply impressed were his auditors: A learned man is the Judge. He knows the law.

A practical man is the Judge. He knows peasant life, too. This is manifest in the informal talk that follows on the moot questions of the village: why boys steal grain; why families are breaking up; why daughters-in-law have become unmanageable. Homely, colloquial, to the point. The peasants were delighted. The cry, *"Pravilno! Pravilno!"* ("Right! Right!") grew louder and louder.

The Judge had attained his end. The competence of the Court had been established.

Meanwhile Lopukhov individualized for me some outstanding figures in the roaring, surging peasant mass.

Andrew Kooznetzov, the biggest *kvas* drinker. Zotey, the strongest man: getting under the belly of a horse and clutching the four legs together, he carried it out of the stable. Babinkov, a Russian southpaw, his left fist a battering ram that always smashes a way to victory in the wall-on-wall fighting. Boodilin, one-time hawker of reserved seats in Paradise to the Mordvinians—"Few places left; buy now!" Gregory Isachev, for thirty years the chief chosen by the village for bribing officials; he never met a judge, surveyor, or *chin-*

ovnik he couldn't give a present to for the general weal of the village—some Commissars to his credit, too. Jacob Beloogin, renowned horse thief, but never caught at it. Nikolai Kolgin, champion *samogon* distiller, his stuff eighty per cent strong. Vassily Lopukhov, who wants the return of monarchy: "The birds," he says, "have a tsar—the eagle; the bees a queen; even the geese a *vozhaty*." Isaac Emelianov, breathing slaughter against the Orthodox priest who ran away with the Whites to Siberia and now lives in a neighboring parish. Isaac says, "Let the priest show his head in Pine Tar and I will kill him." Metrophanov, hell-roaring cavalryman, soured against Moscow because it doesn't declare war on somebody—Poland, China, Africa, it's all the same to him.

In the sea of peasant gray was one fleck of vivid color, the new red-slashed uniform of the "militioner." He was a singularly aloof individual. Only his uniform to indicate that he had any connection with the Court and with the prisoners. In reality there were no prisoners. For in a Russian village one's share of the land is more binding than bail or prison bars. The procedure is very simple. An inspector investigates, draws up a protocol; the accused is notified when to appear for trial.

Everything is ready. Khonin introduces the cojudges (*zasedateli*), the peasants Kootishev and Damitov, who, as they are drawn from another village, Boltinovka, are assumed to be without partiality or prejudice. He explains that he acts as President of the Court, the cojudges having equal powers with himself. He declares the court open and calls the first case.

IV

"Gorbooshev—Anisim Simonovitch."

"Birthplace?"

"Pine Tar Village."

"Age?"

"Thirty-three."

"Married?"

"Yes."

"Property?"

"Boots and clothes I stand up in."

"Do you challenge any member of the Court?

"No."

"Do you have confidence in your judges to give you a fair trial?"

"I do."

Gorbooshev has a peasant's body, big, well built. A peasant's face, broad and smiling. But in voice and bearing is all the urbanity of a man of affairs. And so he is—or was. One-time Tsar officer, one-time Red Commander, one-time Communist, one-time Moscow Co-operator. Now standing before the bar of Pine Tar Village.

Drunk in the Khvalynsk market. Singing drunk on the Volga steamer. Sprawling drunk on the herring wharf at Volsk. But what of that? In Russia a man preserves the inalienable right to get drunk. Gorbooshev has inherited rights as well. He comes from a long line of notorious drinkers. His father, a most religious man,—compelling his family every morning to rise at three o'clock and pray before his forty ikons until five,—was a drunkard. So were his grandfather and great-grandfather. Gorbooshev's appetite has come down a long way and grown in the coming.

It is not drunkenness, however, that Gorbooshev is charged with, but his drinking up nine hundred rubles of the Pine Tar Coöperative, of which he was president and buyer. Sometimes it was a whiff from a *samogon* still that started up his thirst. Sometimes private traders primed the willing victim with vodka, and he sold them the wares of the Coöperative cheap in order to get money for more vodka.

All these exploits Gorbooshev explains in detail. He palliates nothing, conceals nothing, confesses all. All so objectively that it might be the misdeeds and debauches of some one else he is describing—so completely identifying himself with the community that he actually gets to grieving with it over the misfortune of having such a president. Their affliction is his affliction. And by a reverse process his weakness is their weakness. All of them—somehow the Court, too, whom he addresses as "Comrade judges"—are in the muck together, and somehow all together they must get out of it.

Now the defender, Vasiyev. He shows that Gorbooshev's vodka spreeing was not unmitigated evil. True, certain traders plied him with vodka for their ends; but he in turn plied other traders with vodka, selling them onions at fifty kopecks above the market price, on this one deal alone making an extra profit of sixteen hundred rubles for the Pine Tar onion growers.

Next the prosecutor, Bolshakov. He picks up the onions and, so to speak, rubs them into the defender's eyes. He shows that the onion buyers Gorbooshev corrupted were agents of the main Coöperative. "Out of the main Coöperative come all our goods; out of this corruption come higher prices. Cloth leaving Moscow at thirty kopecks brings fifty kopecks in Pine Tar—thanks to these criminals. As once horse stealing was epidemic in the village, now it is Coöperative stealing. Moscow cries

out, 'Stop these thieves!' There they stopped
them with bullets, shooting sixteen of these
enemies of the Soviet. We don't ask you to
shoot Gorbooshev, but to put him where such
birds belong—in a cage."

Acid, stinging words, taking the smile off the
face of Gorbooshev. Like a great hurt child, he
stands fingering the Lenin badge on his coat.

"Enemy of the Soviet?" Didn't he twenty
times risk his life for that Soviet, leading his
troops against the Whites? "Criminal?"
Wasn't it he who put his feeble Coöperative on
its feet, raising its capital from one hundred
to twelve thousand rubles? "Thief?" He
hadn't forged any documents, falsified any ac-
counts. True, he took a little money. Not for
his pocket, but for his throat, to slake the burning thirst there. And everybody else's thirst
also.

"If he had only one bottle of vodka, he
would give you half of it," whispers a peasant
to me. Greater love hath no man than this.

"How am I to blame? With the same

thirst, in the same position, anybody might have done the same." That's the way he feels. And that's the way most of the peasants feel, touched with pity when Gorbooshev, discouraged by the grilling, gives it up and throws himself upon the mercy of the Court. Had he turned round and thrown himself upon the mercy of the peasants, the Court in all probability would have been assailed by a storm of voices crying, "Forgive! Forgive!" Knowing his peasants, Gorbooshev knows this well. He has fallen a long way, but not so far as this.

The case is closed. The judges retire to prepare the verdict. There are calls from the floor: "The American! The American! Tell us about your land across the sea!"

I compare the two countries, peoples and food, incidentally touching on the relative leanness of Americans. A voice calls out: "If, as you say, the Americans are thinner than we are, why is it that you, citizen Williams, are so full-blooded?" (*Polnokrovny*—polite word for "fat.")

I explain: "It's because I've been in Russia three years and eaten much bread and *kasha*."

"And drunk much vodka and *samogon*," mumbles a *mujik* in the center.

I break to them the dread news that in American all liquor—vodka, whiskey, wine, beer—is forbidden. A general groan, and an old man rising to ask, "Is this the reason, then, comrade, you came to live with us in Russia?"

"And if it is a free country," puts in another, "why do they stop vodka?"

One reason I offer is the vast number of factories, trains, and automobiles in America. A worker a little unsteady from alcohol may kill many people and destroy valuable machines.

"That means, brother *mujiks*," shouts a voice from the back, "if we are going to have tractors we must give up vodka."

Bursts of laughter and cries of "Never! Never!"

Our pleasant colloquy is interrupted by the

cry: "The Court assembles!" The peasants rise, and Khonin reads the verdict:—

"In the name of the Russian Socialist Federated Soviet Republics, the People's Court of the Sixth District [and so forth], hearing the case of Gorbooshev, age thirty-three [and so forth], for misappropriation of funds [and so forth], declares him guilty, and sentences him to one year in prison. But taking into consideration his services in organizing the Coöperative, his frank confession [and so forth], ten months of this term are made conditional. Two months to serve."

From the formal decision the Judge at once passes to an informal interpretation. "We bring in a sentence of guilty on one man. It might well be a sentence of guilty on a thousand men—upon all of you. You saw your president drinking. Some of you drank with him. You knew vodka costs money. You knew where he got it. But you did nothing about it. Never shall we have social institu-

tions until we have social responsibility."
Pointing the moral of the strong man broken
by strong drink, he declares a recess.

Now the peasants' verdict on the verdict.

"Too hard! Sitting in a cage—what good
will that do?" Against this majority a few
voices declare the sentence too soft. Gorbooshev's wife thinks he ought to have a year.
Gorbooshev himself thinks it about right. At
any rate, he can't get anything to drink for two
months.

v

"Goorlev!" calls the secretary clerk.

An overcoatless peasant, carrying a silver-
headed cane, steps forward. He is charged
with "insulting the Government" in the person of five members of the Soviet of Yelkhovka,
a near-by village. They testify that he called
them "impostors, bandits, and thieves," and
that when they refused his demands he cried
out: "I'm a Communist, and I'll show you who
runs Russia." This is an old feud. Even here

the five peasants keep slyly baiting hot-tempered Goorlev. Maybe they will provoke another explosion.

"They are all *koolaks* conspiring against me!" he declares. Swathed in enormous *tooloops*, they do have a distinctly kulak look. But it turns out that not one has more than a single horse or two cows. They are "middle" peasants. Beaten on point after point, the Communist calls up his record in the Revolution. While these five skulked at home, he fought. "Are not my services to be taken into consideration?"

"When you stand before a commission of the Communist Party, they are," replies the Judge; "but not here. This is a Soviet court. In it you stand like any other citizen."

The Court's verdict, however, is inconsistent with this statement. "Fifteen days of compulsory labor. *Taking into account that Goorlev is a Communist*, thirty days extra. A copy of this sentence to be sent to the Party."

Next came two lads up for insulting a girl.

They had painted her door with tar—in a Russian village no slur is worse than this. As is smeared the peasant's door, so is smeared the peasant's daughter. The culprits, frightened, declare they will never do it again. They are let off with a lecture on hooliganism and staying up all night till rooster crow.

Next, a village *baba* who performed criminal operations. Wires and spindles were her surgical instruments. Taking court exhibit **A**, a bent, rusted knitting needle, which she used in her last case, the Judge asked:—

"Is this clean?"

"According to us—clean."

"Where did you keep the needle?"

"On the ikon shelf."

"Did you ever disinfect it before using?"

"Sometimes sprinkled it with holy water."

She is given six months, but when she promises to cease the practice, sentence is made conditional.

"Now," says the Judge, "let us look into this evil. We hold that the right to bear a child or not rests with the woman. If she is sick, or has too large a family, or there is dire necessity, she can come to the Khvalynsk hospital, where skilled physicians will perform the operation free. But how is it generally done? By ignorant *babas* like this one, often crippling or killing the mothers. Who is to blame for that? You men—you fathers. A girl goes 'walking'; nature takes her course. Something happens. The frightened girl must hide it or be driven from home, beaten half to death by her father. But did none of you men go walking before you were married? Do you drive your sons from home, beat them half to death, when they go walking? How is the woman more to blame than the man? Equal rights for all. This is the Soviet position. The village too must come to this."

VI

Through such homilies the Judge attains one of the objects set before the People's Court. It becomes a school of citizenship. When the attention of the hearers flagged, he would refresh the courtroom—and himself—with a story. Most of the stories were like the following, ironic reflections upon the old order.

In Ivanovka Village the old *starosta* was in trouble over the taxes. One night the inspector, a fierce, mustached, foot-stamping giant, came driving up in his *troika*.

Without seeing the *starosta*, he put up at the pope's house. A sleepless night for the already worried *starosta*. Worse still, in the morning a poor *mujik* tried to commit suicide by hanging himself in his shed. He was cut down, still breathing, and the *starosta*, terribly wrought up, ran off to the inspector to report. Dripping sweat, cap in hand, he stood quaking before the door for a long time, not daring to knock. Finally, crossing himself, he pushed it open, thrust his white head in, and, coughing slightly to attract attention, mumbled:—

"Your Highness, I'm the *starosta*."

"Well!" roared the inspector, turning to him.

"Please, sir, there is a *mujik* who just hanged himself out there."

"What did you do?"

"We took him down, Your Highness."

"Took him down?" bellowed the inspector, pounding the table. "*Svoloch*, pig! By what right? You should have placed guards and reported to the authorities. I'll teach you—"

But the *starosta* was off to the shed, where he found the *mujik* just gaining consciousness. Taking on the tone and manner of the inspector, he roared to the crowd: "*Svoloch*, pigs! Go home! Disperse! And you guards pick up the man and hang him again."

"But he's alive!" they protested.

"No matter. The inspector has commanded it. Hang him up, and you guards stand at attention."

Hardly was the gasping victim strung up when the inspector arrived on the scene.

"Your Highness," said the *starosta*, again crossing himself and bending low, "he begged not to be hung up. But we did it just as Your Highness ordered."

The story is not so fantastic as might seem. As Nastyrev, a great peasant jurist, says: "In the eyes of the *mujik*, law is something terrible, mysterious, incomprehensible, in the name of which the Government terrorizes, abuses, and mutilates, whips out arrears in taxes, exiles to Siberia, disembowels corpses, pulls down houses, kills stock, drafts into the army, *ad infinitum*." And Kocharovsky, another old authority on peasant life, says, "The rôle of law in the life of the peasant is something similar to a dreadful natural phenomenon; the purpose of it is not understood, but its power is felt to be irresistible."

Every old peasant knows how the officers of the law, arbitrary and aloof and sacrosanct, used to encourage a blind submission to authority, a slavish groveling before them.

VII

In glaring contrast to this old officialdom was the conduct of the new personnel, removing from the court every formality except rising to hear the verdict; wearing no insignia of party or office, unless the red worsted scrolls on the Judge's Novgorod felt boots may be accounted such; sharing with the peasants the decisions and application of the law; taking them into the secret of the making of laws and of judges.

"How did you become a judge?" asked the old Agaphonov.

"The Party told me to go and be a judge. 'How can I?' I asked. 'Simple enough,' they answered. 'Start judging, and you will be a judge.' So I did—and here I am."

All barriers with the Judge were down. He made himself utterly accessible. Each day he held court till seven. Then in our quarters a samovar court till midnight, son Jacob dispensing tea, the Judge dispensing stories and counsel to all who came.

It is like a confessional. A newly married soldier suddenly remembering he has a second wife in the Ukraine. A young Tartar bumping his wife off his wagon and stove in order to bring on a miscarriage. Another girl with child. Shall she give birth to it out of wedlock?

"Of course," says the Judge.

"But it has no means of support," says the girl.

"It has a father, hasn't it?" says the Judge. "If he won't pay, tell him you will bring him into court and make him."

Rarely he thus calls up the strong arm of the law, always offering services of mediation, reconciling hastily married and hastily repentant youth, hot-tempered sons with despotic fathers, and to all would-be litigants quoting the proverb, "Don't go into the courts. The bast shoe will cost more than the felt boot."

All this good fellowship of the Judge the younger generation accepts in a natural, matter-of-fact way. But the elders cannot get out of their heads the ancient conception of a judge.

One night came a delegation of four, the spokesman the very image of Ilya Moorometz in the Tretyakov Gallery. With beard sweeping the floor as he bowed, he began with the ancient formula of address to officials:—

"Your Highness!"

"S-sh! Hush!" mumbled the others, tugging at his coat. This salutation they knew wasn't right. But what is right?

"Mister!"

"Comrade!"

"Citizen!"

Each salutation, old and new, they try in turn, while the Judge keeps repeating, "Sit down!" He has to force them into the chairs. But they could not be at ease. For with them holds strong the old idea of a judge as a dignitary of great power, and incidentally of great venality. A personage to be feared—and to be bribed.

"A gift to the judge, the case is decided," goes an old Russian proverb. Every old peas-

ant knows that, well remembering the old officials junketing with the richer peasants at the
Elder's house. There behind the closed doors,
around a demijohn of vodka, many cases were
decided, generally in favor of the owner of
the demijohn or the man who kept it filled.

Over in Yelshanka another Ilya Moorometz,
carrying on the old tradition, slipped the Judge
a bottle of vodka. Khonin brought the bottle
to court, placed it on the table, and told the
peasants what had happened.

"I've got the vodka, and, according to Stat-
ute 114 of the Criminal Code, the giver gets one
year in prison. However, let him go. He was
raised in the old ways. But we want new ways.
We Communists are trying to clean out the dis-
honest and put in the honest; then you come
around trying to corrupt us. Men are weak.
So long as there are peasant bribe-givers, there
will be official bribe-takers. To your cry, 'Give
us honest officials!' we answer, 'Give us honest
peasants.' "

But Khonin has no cause to complain about

his constituency. To a people nurtured in the institutions of autocracy, he comes with the most ultrademocratic of institutions. To a people for centuries kept aloof and in fear of their officials, he comes with ultra *camaraderie*, hands down and defenseless. I was on the lookout for some one to presume upon this with a gratuitous familiarity, some back-slipping act of rustic boorishness. But there was none. These peasants were worthy of the democracy they were getting. The more he democratized his bearing, the more respect and deference he received. Before one's eyes one could watch the rise of the authority of the Court and the prestige of the Soviet.

Conversely, too, one may see the authority of the ancient faith and the prestige of the old institutions failing. Each trip has its devastating effect. One expedition of the Judge into the village is about equal to one ton of propaganda literature.

"Come to supper!" "Comrade Judge, come over and we'll set up a samovar." Scores of these invitations besiege him. So the Judge enters into the homes of the strictest sectarians, to whom any one not an Old Believer is unclean, a "worldly" man who contaminates even the dishes out of which he eats. Afterward they must be broken to pieces, or cleansed by a long ceremonial. When an Old Believer *baba* serves the Judge a plate of cabbage, he warns her, "It will cost you forty *epitoms* or forty kopecks to get a new plate."

But she laughs. Isn't the Judge for women? Hasn't he praised the "milk and blood" cheeks of her ten-year-old Marusya? Somehow the Judge is one of their own, and to him the religious interdictions do not apply. So the breach in the old customs is made. Maybe not always for the common good.

Smoking, for example. As hats for women and razors for men, so tobacco in the Old Believers' code is forbidden to all. And the Judge smokes. Four years ago he took up the habit, but he carries it on with all the zeal of a new convert. In the intermission after the Gorbooshev case, he asked the peasants:—

"Now will you let me take a smoke?"

"Smoke! Smoke!" was the loud reply.

At his quarters he always laid the box of Cannon cigarettes on the table. Anybody might take one. But, as befitting Old Believers, no one did. So stood their forbears against tobacco in the days of Peter the Great; so stand their sons to-day. Thus I wrote it down, and thus my testimony would stand had I not observed one night Foma Karpovitch strangely edging his cap over to the box. Presently some cigarettes disappeared. Then Foma disappeared.

A few minutes later I opened the door of the cow shed to find three forty-year-old *mujiks* coughing and blowing smoke through their beards. They tried to look innocent, then laughed, and, like bad boys caught smoking in the barn, swore me not to tell.

"*Papasha*," said Foma, "would abuse us

dreadfully; maybe they would try us before the church." Foma, however, was not to be caught napping. His line of defense was all laid out. The Old Believers' interdiction against smoking is based on the text, "Not that which goeth into the mouth defileth a man; but that which cometh out of the mouth, this defileth a man."

"Look!" said Foma, emitting a stream of smoke through his nostrils to the great admiration of his fellow accomplices. "It doesn't come out of my mouth, but out of my nose."

"Evidently the making of a first-class judge in Foma," was Khonin's comment when I told him the story.

A keen sense of the comic spirit in life has the Judge. It makes him look at all things humorously, objectively—even judges.

"To what end fines and jails?" he philosophized. "How ridiculous to make men good by doing them evil! How presumptuous to make one man arbiter of the fate of his fellow men!"

These are the ideas of Tolstoy, Hugo, Zola,

picked up in youth, reflected now in his conversation. Once I heard a public outburst of them. It was at Popovka, where he set forth the theory of Soviet law:—

Not rigid framework into which the peasant must fit his life, but flexible forms, adjusting themselves to the central practice and interest of the peasants. Not codes springing readymade from the brains of autocratic rulers, but rules of life drawn up by the people themselves. Followed a referendum upon the proposed change in the marriage code: to declare all marriages legally valid, whether registered in the Soviet or not. Incidentally, though this would raise the status of Church marriages, ninety-five per cent of the peasants voted against it.

Now rose the peasant Borodin, enthusiastically exclaiming, "Who would ever dream that the Court would travel out to us, that it would consult with us about the laws? I tell you, brother *mujiks*, that this is good!"

Khonin rose, saying, "And I will tell you something better. That is, the day will come when there will be no need for a court to come to you—when there will be no militia or codes or jails; no judges, no prosecutors."

This is Khonin the dreamer, indulging in visions of the Communist society to be. Khonin the realist knows that, in the society that is, the Court must continue to function; that his task is to make it function more effectively, to make himself more efficient. That's the reason why, at the call of the Party, this winter, he is reluctantly leaving his village for Saratov, to take a year's course of study to fill up the gaps in his knowledge.

IX

WHO BURNED THE KOCHOOBEY
PALACE AND WHY?

IX

WHO BURNED THE KOCHOOBEY PALACE AND WHY?

But Kochoobey was rich and proud,
Not in his long-maned horses,
Nor the gold tribute of the Crimean Hordes
Nor in his fertile farms,
But in his beautiful daughter.

THUS Pushkin's famous poem, *Poltava*, begins, recounting the glories of the famous Kochoobeys. My guide pointed out the great oak under which the old Mazepa made love to that "beautiful daughter," Maria. That is about all that remains intact of the great estate that lies on the edge of Dikanka village. The rest is ruins.

A long tumbling brick wall; this was once the deer-park. A stagnant pond out of which statues thrust up broken arms and legs; this was the lake, once dotted white with swans. The butt of a palm tree crowning a cinder-heap; this was the orangery. A line of fire-gutted buildings; these were the stables of the long-maned racing horses. Some ring bolts in a pile of bricks; these chained the hunting pack, whose cries one time wakened the countryside.

Beyond this desolation, past great green spaces, stood the glistening white portico of the palace, columns and walls so clean and straight it seemed the palace was intact. But it was only a white shell enclosing a burnt brick and tangled débris. After the fire came the spoilers, sacking it to the last bolt and window frame. Then came the treasure hunters. Last of all the vandals.

"Before and after the fire." Thus local history is reckoned from that unforgettable

night in the winter 1919, when a red tongue of
fire leaped out of the dark, climbed about the
tops of the trees, grew into a pillar of flame,
fountaining into the sky, mahogany, paintings,
rugs and tapestries. Two nights and a day it
frightened and fascinated the countryside for
fifty miles round. A magnificent conflagration
—the funeral pyre of feudalism.

One of the peasants told me how it happened: "A band of partisans rode out of the
forest one day and camped on the grounds.
At night we saw them suddenly saddle and
gallop away. An hour later the palace was
flaming."

"Yes, that's the way it started," affirmed a
second, "the partisans set it afire."

Thus I heard the story from a score of peasants, and so I would have recorded it had not
the palace overseer one time, in talking about
the library, remarked: "That's probably where
the fire began. Some boys playing there may
have knocked a lighted candle into the papers."

Both versions I related to a Poltava cattle-dealer. "Neither boys nor partisans," said he, "it was the peasants themselves who fired the palace. They laid straw in the cellar and waited their opportunity. The partisans out of the forest gave it to them. As they rode away the peasants touched it off. So they escape responsibility, always saying, 'The partisans did it!'" This I take to be the true version.

At any rate one thing is very clear. I never heard one peasant regret that the palace was gone. But why were they glad? And to what extent was it the sweet sense of gratified revenge against the Kochoobeys?

Against the prince himself I could not find particular ill-will. He was hard working, tramped around in worn-out shoes, greeted everybody affably, refused a Court Minister's portfolio, saying, "I can't be always kissing ladies' hands." Quite a democrat. He was easy on his peasants, renting out his land for seven rubles a *dessyatine* when it was twelve elsewhere, in slack season keeping their horses busy hauling at four kopecks a *pood*.

For the son there was warm feeling. "Maybe you'll meet him in London or Paris," said a young peasant to me. "He was a good fellow and a wizard with the stringed instruments. Tell him to come back and we'll make him chief commissar of our Balalaika Club."

For the brother, a magnificent drinker, there was admiration. He drank himself fat and bankrupt, then took to wife Stolypin's niece with a seven million ruble dowry.

It was on the Princess that the anger of the peasants converged. Evidence of this I found on a marble pillar in the big pasture. Out of a camp-fire some shepherd had drawn a lop-eared, three-breasted lady with a long spear-pointed tail. Below in strong Ukrainian "All Princesses! To hell with them!" Maybe this rustic artist had once been lashed off the place by the Princess' tongue. Or he had not lifted his cap to her. Homage to caste and rank she demanded at all costs. Let the *mujik* be rolling drunk; let him beat his wife; but let him be deferential. Then all was forgiven. But damned forever was the wretch who once mistook her for the veterinary's wife.

Terrorist and termagant, but a great lover of animals—a skilled horsewoman, a devotee to dogs, her affection particularly concentrated on a little white pet terrier, Looloo. The dog had her own cook, wardrobe and servant. When Looloo died the grief-stricken Princess had an island made in the lake, set with shrubs and flowers.

"There's where the bitch buried her bitch," said our peasant guide, pointing to the lake below. "Looloo's Island we had to call it. A whole island for a dog. And to us she grudged a crust of bread, a log of fire-wood, or even to put foot on her estate."

"She-devil! Maybe now she would like a stick of fire wood herself. She'd have to ask for it. So Princess, you would like to walk through the estate?" His voice and manner

were now in droll imitation of her. "Sorry,
tovarisch Princess, you'll have to go back and
get permission from the Soviet."

The war, it seemed, softened or scared her
and she took to giving presents to the conscripts.
"When I was enlisted," said young Cheiben,
"she called me to the palace and gave me a ten
ruble gold piece. 'Brave boy,' she said, 'go
fight for your fatherland and freedom!'

"And sure enough," continued Cheiben, "I
got a certain amount of both. I'm going to
curse the Soviet to-day about the taxes—that's
freedom. As for fatherland, I've got fifteen
dessyatines of the Kochoobey estate."

Cheiben was vengeful, but ironically, pleas-
antly so. Bitter shrilled the vengeance in an
old soldier describing the raid on the mausoleum of Sergius Victorovitch Kochoobey:
"First we smashed the stone coffin, then the
oak and the zinc."

"Maybe it was the gold cross around his
neck, the jewels and money you were after?"
I suggested.

"No!" said the old man scornfully. "I was after the old devil himself. He stole the land from my fathers. God curse his soul!" he screamed, with hate-contorted face making a deep slashing stab with his crutch. "I put a knife through his chest."

Vengeance against even the dead. Not blind, indiscriminate, however, but directed against those who had injured them. The bones of Leo Victorovitch lie undisturbed; he gave the forest to the village. Sergius Victorovitch took the forest back; it was his tomb that was desecrated. It was into his ribs that this old soldier savagely thrust his knife.

Revenge played its part in the palace burning. But, to my mind, a small part. The fact remains that, for two years after the outbreak of the Revolution, the palace was untouched. It was as if the peasants said to it: "Remember, in the old days, you have been a source of insult and injury to us. But for these sins of the past we will not punish you. We put you on good behavior." Unfortunately the palace did not mend its ways. Indeed it became worse. With the return of the Whites, one time, came the former superintendent, imposing a levy of one hundred and sixty thousand rubles on the peasants. To their remonstrations he replied: "Be thankful it is so little. Some day, on your knees, at the gates, you will be begging a little bran to stop the gnawing in your bellies."

Yet, such was the nature of the palace, now humiliating them, now threatening hunger and death. Here is the letter of a runaway landlord of Tula to his peasants:

"*Brother Mujiks:* Go on as you have begun. Divide all the furnishings of my manor-house. Take my cattle and the hay to feed them with. One thing I ask of you! Don't chop down my lime trees. These I will need to hang you on when I return. . . ."

"*When I return!* Damn him!" Let there be nothing to return to. They hewed the lime-trees down.

So it was in Yurievskaya. When the landlord Kovalevsky fled, the peasants settled old scores with the manager and divided up the furnishings and live stock. Then came the Skoropadsky Government (the Whites) and an officer, appearing before the Peasant Committee, announced:

"Sheep, cows, beds, books, carpets—back to Sir Kovalevsky. He who has eaten the sheep, get into the skin and crawl back on all fours himself!" He led his finger twice around the face of his watch. "Twenty-four hours—the time limit! If one sack of corn, one spoon, one hen is missing . . . this!" The officer drew his finger across his throat. "And this!" He struck a match, meaning the village would be fired.

Dawn next day and over the long road leading to the estate stood great dust clouds, beaten up by the wheat and hay laden wagons, by the hoofs of the bleating, neighing, grunting, bellowing beasts, while through the tangle stumbled women with mirrors, old men with birdcages, boys with wagon-wheels, plows and vases. Everything and everybody, for the way was long, the time was short and the big guns were trained upon the village.

Forward they pressed to the gates from which two lines of soldiers stretched to the manor-house. Down this lane of bayonets the peasants passed, each to lay his loot at the feet of Kovalevsky.

"It was like the great Judgment Day," said a peasant, "each of us bringing his own sins, piling them on the heap. When the Whites left a second time we touched nothing. We burned the palace down."

"Why didn't you take the things again? There was no one to stop you."

"Take them again," he soliloquized. "Maybe give them back again. Go through hell again? No, we couldn't do that!"

In flames and smoke they blotted out the scene of their humiliation, their degradations of the past. More than that, by this act they were blotting out the humiliations that might be, the degradations of the future. Wiping them out forever.

So it was with the palace of the Kochoobeys, standing above the village. Menacing, arbitrary, pregnant with evil. As Leo, the good Kochoobey, gave way to Sergius the bad, so the kindly prince might give way to the unbridled Princess, the Princess to some one worse. Then what new affronts, insults and injuries? The ruins of the palace were the assurance that these things should not be. In this guarantee of the future, more than in the sweet sense of gratified revenge for the past, lies the general peasant satisfaction over its destruction.

Of course, there was another and more basic reason for this satisfaction. Anybody with the slightest knowledge of the peasants, and the object which they sought to attain through the Revolution, knows what this is. How fully, magnificently the Revolution realized that object I never understood until I met Pitrenko.

X

AMERICA COMES TO DIKANKA

X

AMERICA COMES TO DIKANKA

ALEXANDER ANDREEVITCH PITRENKO introduced himself one morning in the Dikanka bazaar, exclaiming: "I've got a letter from America. From the Silver Republic!" Taken aback for a moment, then I understood—it was from the Argentine Republic. From Buenos Ayres, his brother was writing: "Now is the time to come. A new section is opening up. You can buy land for twenty rubles an acre."

All his life Alexander Andreevitch Pitrenko had lived cramped up on one acre of land. All his life he had dreamed of wide expanses, long black furrows turning behind a yoke of cream-colored oxen, wide pasture for the oxen to graze upon. Always these lands were in America. For him America was just another word for land. Years ago his brother had gone away, while here in Dikanka he had awaited a letter almost breathlessly. Now it had come telling of new ranches opening to settlers, telling Alexander Andreevitch to come along.

"When are you going?" I asked him.

"I'm not going at all," he answered. "I don't have to go to America. America has come to me."

Instead of journeying ten thousands of miles across seas, Alexander Andreevitch had only to cross the road to the Soviet Land Bureau. Here was his dream come true. Land, not at low prices—but for the asking, for nothing at all—good land too, better than in America, rich black loam.

He had gotten fifteen acres of it, an orchard, three years' exemption from all taxes. So, only ten versts away from his old home, he became a settler and in a dugout sodden with grass he lived like a pioneer. Now and then a strange pioneer loneliness came upon him, relieved by a drive down to the village.

Around Dikanka hundreds of Pitrenkos had been set up with a complete farm, thousands had added to their holdings.

To the peasants, the Revolution was an act of Creation. Fire, storm, blaze and thunder of cannons—the convulsion of a continent—then out of this chaos, land emerging, vast areas of it and theirs to have and to hold.

To this end the peasant had battled for centuries, fighting under the banners raised by the Pugachevs and Stenka Razins, suffering floggings and exiles, beaten back again and again, but through the darkest nights of Russian reaction, ever dreaming of the day when the land would be his. And now it was his. The dream was reality. Forty million *dessyatines*—an area as large as England—had passed into his hands. Every peasant in the Ukraine nearly doubled his holding. Fifty-five per cent of the land belonged to the peasant. Then the Revolution and ninety-six per cent of it was his.

"The lands of the crown, the monasteries and the landlord, are hereby declared the property of the nation forever." Thus reads the land decree passed on the night of November 7, 1917, while the smoke had hardly died from the guns of the Aurora firing over the Winter Palace. Thus the miracle is recorded.

Alongside of this stupendous fact goes another almost as stupendous—the passing over of the fact in silence. One would think that pæans of joy would signalize such magnificent realization of their hopes. Instead of that, a silence almost universal. Out of thousands of peasants whom I have picked up in casual conversation, I can count upon my fingers the Pitrenkos who volunteered, "I got a *dessyatine* of land out of the Revolution." All the others sedulously concealed it. As in Dikanka, so elsewhere.

There was the loquacious basket weaver from Novgorod, with whom I had converse for many

months. This barefooted *batrak* had received
a ten-*dessyatine khutor*, as I learned a year
later and accidentally. From him not a word.

There is the garden village of Zhoozhin,
three versts from Moscow, where the peasants
have increased their holdings two, three, and
even five fold. From them you may hear long
discourse about fruit stealers, bad roads, lazi-
ness of laborers—everything under heaven.
But about their rich inheritance, never a hint.

There are the peasants down in the bread-
basket of the world—the Volga basin. How
often, on the ferry gliding across the river, they
have told me dismal tales of the *mgla*, the
Dryer (*Sookhoyer*), the grasshopper invasion,
the blunders of the state grain buyers and
Soviet agronomists. But the land carved out
for them of the Medem, Davidov, Dacboron-
sky estates, and out of the *kulak* tracts—rich
black steppe soil in which the wheat grows rank
like weeds—about this never a word. Never
a word until they see that I am not an innocent. Then they will admit it, but with reser-

vations and evasions, concealing the amount of their gain.

Is this the silence of dread? The fear that he may have to return the land and pay with stripes on his back for taking it? In the early years of the Revolution there were certain peasants whom nothing could induce to settle on the landlord's estates. But now this plays no part, for the peasant is pretty well convinced that the landlord has gone to stay.

The real reason for this silence one must find in the peculiar peasant minds and conceptions. First of all his attitude towards land and its ownership. The American would say simply enough: "The land belongs to him who owns it." The Russian peasant says: "The land belongs to him who works it." In the words of the delegate to the Peasant Congress of 1905. "Land is the gift of God like air and water. Only he who applies his labor to it should have it, each according to his needs." This is the only fundamental inviolate right, all other claims are fictitious. Why then make a fuss over the getting of his simple rights?

Furthermore why should he make great ado over the restitution of that which was stolen from him? Sometimes it was stolen in the grand manner of Ekaterina bestowing largesses upon her lovers.

Sometimes it was piecemeal by trickery as with the old Kochoobey. "Himself a Cossack, he robbed even the Cossacks." When troops from the north were billeted on the village, good order was maintained in the houses of Kochoobey's serfs, while in the houses of the poor Cossacks the soldiers caroused, plundered and violated at will. A Cossack would go to Kochoobey protesting:

"Why come to me?" the old Prince would say. "I can protect only my own peasants."

"Make me one of yours then!" the victim would plead.

His name was accordingly written down in "the book"—with his name went his land.

Thus by indirect action the boundaries of the Prince were extended five, ten or fifty *dessyatines*.

Sometimes it was direct action as in the case of Cheiben, of the ten ruble gold piece, related to me. "My great grandfather had fifteen *dessyatines* of woodland which took the eye of the old Prince. One morning great-grand-father went out to chop down trees and found forest guards there who told him to keep off. When he wouldn't, they gave him the *nagaika* —five strokes a *dessyatine*. It's my land now and I've got a *nagaika* for any Kochoobey who steps on it."

The Revolution was the repatriation of the soil. The Cheibens were simply coming into their own. Why then should they break forth into pæans of praise for getting that which by every natural and legal right was theirs? Especially when they had redeemed it in the battle and blood of seven years' civil war.

It is the Communist, of course, who directed this battle and led it to success. The peasant knows this very well. It is the basis of a deep fundamental allegiance to the Communist. It is deep in his consciousness, though it may not be upon his lips. So the peasant deceives the foreigner—sometimes even the Communist— and always the great *emigrés* statesmen of Paris, Prague and London think that because the peasant doesn't express gratitude he doesn't feel it; because he isn't loud in his loyalty he doesn't have it; fools, deceiving themselves because they want to be deceived. Do they think that the peasant can ever forget the political party that put forty million *dessyatines* of land under his feet?

Besides the peasant's conviction that in obtaining the land he is obtaining only his rights, there is another consideration that holds him back from breaking forth into psalms of rejoicing, and particularly restrains him from thanksgiving to the Communist. In the craftiness of his peasant soul he knows that benefits received mean obligations incurred—duties to fulfill—services to perform—to acknowledge

[249]

favors is to assume responsibilities. Better then say nothing about these benefits. Better not talk about what the Revolution has given him, but what it is taking away from him. Better concentrate, for example, on taxes.

That's what Dibenko was doing one morning I came into the Soviet. Taxes were robbery. The Soviet, brigands! He called on me as an American to behold in him a man brought to ruin. I stopped his eloquence with the curt question:

"How much land, Dibenko, did you have before the Revolution?"

"None!" was his reluctant answer.

"How many *dessyatines* now?"

"Twelve," more reluctantly.

"How much a *dessyatine* is it worth? If you had had to buy it now, how much would you have had to pay?"

Dibenko tried to wriggle away, but I pinned him down. He had to admit that his land was the best black loam—worth four hundred rubles a *dessyatine* at the lowest estimate—four thousand, eight hundred rubles it would have cost him. And his taxes were forty-six rubles! Not one per cent interest on the value of his land received gratis.

"Now honestly, Dibenko," I asked him, taking him aside, "about the land, why is it that you never say a word?"

"Why should I?" he laughed. "I've got as much as I want. The land isn't troubling me. I'm going to talk about what is troubling me."

Thus all over the Soviet Union the peasants, like Dibenko, as deliberate policy are keeping to the front their grievances. In meeting, *izba*, boat, train, one can hear them chanting the litany of their woes: high taxes, high prices, of city goods, low prices on grain, lack of horses, misdeeds of Communists and the Soviet —all the evils that, justly or unjustly, have been laid to the account of the Revolution.

Scarcely a hint from the peasants about benefits received from the Revolution: deliverance from servile obedience to officers and landlords; the right to his own language, culture and religion; the path of learning cleared for him right into the university; the right of free and unlimited criticism; the shortening of war service; the hundreds of new cultural devices; mail ring-posts, *izba* reading rooms, tractors and electricity—and above all, that supreme conquest of the Revolution—the land. Of all this on the lips of the peasant scarcely a word.

But does this mean that he is not fully aware of these conquests of the Revolution, and the political party which helped him achieve them?

If you will, call the peasant crafty, ungrateful, cunning, but do not call him a fool.

XI

THE ABBESS, THE ARCHEOLOGIST
AND THE AGITATOR

XI

THE ABBESS, THE ARCHEOLOGIST
AND THE AGITATOR

A RADIANT June morning on the rolling
plains of Vladimir. Deeper than the white
snow blanket dropped down by winter skies is
the green one in which the land has clothed
itself. The lush green of lusty meadow grass,
the dark green of oat and wheat and barley. A
vast carpet of billowing green shot through
with cornflower blue, silver sheened by the
breezes.

We follow a trail that runs through high
walls of flowering grain, through birch groves

bursting into song, down into little glades drifted deep with daisies, up again on ridges from which the cereal sea sweeps toward the west. And just when our spirits are flagging in the noonday heat, a hill top, and from it a sudden vision of breath-taking beauty. In the white clouds on the far horizon, floating above the vast expanse of shimmering green, a cluster of domes and belfries, high turrets and golden cupolas glittering in the sun.

So unexpected, so entrancing that for the moment I thought it a phantasy, one of those optical illusions that tantalize the thirsty, tired traveler of the desert. But, unlike a mirage, it stood still, grew bigger, bolder in outline, and from one of the belfries came the faint booming of a bell. Not a phantom city in the clouds, but a city set on a hill above the river Kamenka—the ancient city of Suzdal.

In the dim historic past—before Moscow was known—Suzdal was capital of the Northern Slavs, citadel of refugees from raiding hordes and robbers; lustrous with the names of Vassily the Dark, Yurev the Long-armed, Andrew, Lover of God, and with the exploits of the ten thousand marching against Magnus the Swede.

Then the Mongols came rolling over her ramparts; Mahmet tearing the cross from the breast of the Suzdal prince to send as a mocking present to his wife; Suzdal bishops, with bared heads, carrying tribute to the Volga Khans. But out of her blood-stained ashes the city rose again in splendor. The blue falcon fluttering from her walls in welcome to Ivan the Terrible returning in triumph from the conquest of Kazan. Out of Suzdal gates Pozharsky fared forth to drive the Poles from Russia, and into the far corners of the land Suzdal merchants carried the famed products of her painters and weavers.

A vast mausoleum of memories. Long since princes and *boyars* and warriors have turned to dust. Trade and industry have ebbed away. The thriving city has shrunk to a village, the green fields now creeping down the long streets and across the great squares, once echoing to the fanfare of drums and trumpets, the herds go kicking up the dust. Gone the actors in the great dramas. Gone the ancient pomp and pageantry. All gone, save a few hundred cowled and hooded figures and the pilgrims to the shrines in summer. Only in the bazaar, a faint flare up of the old life on market day when the peasants come thronging in.

Still on the green plains of Vladimir, for centuries to come, will stand these massive monuments witnessing to the one time power and splendor of Suzdal: the earth wall against which rolled the Golden Hordes; the vast establishments of the monastic orders; the churches and cathedrals crowded with star-fretted domes, with myriads of cupolas, emerald and gold and Chinese blue.

Some five and thirty mammoth "summer" churches—any one a landmark in an American city—and nestling beside them as many "winter" churches. All of them built for eternity. Not with modern three brick walls, but sixteen bricks deep and often twice or thrice that number. The more bricks, the more glory to God. With like prodigality the interior decorators lavished their gold and paint and lacquer. And everywhere a reek of religious riches and relics.

In the first church we entered, an array of trophies that would put an Italian shrine to shame: blond lock from the Mother of God; a finger of her mother Ann; a piece of the robe of Jesus; wood from His cradle; wisdom tooth of Moses; thumb-nail of Isaiah. In all sixty relics, brought from Byzantium by the first Greek emissaries and imposed upon the credulity of the early Slavs.

In the afternoon our wanderings brought us to the walls of a monastery, rising like red cliffs above the river. Massive bastions and turrets loopholed for cannons and arquebuses proclaimed that these walls were built, not as a symbol of separation from the world and its temptations, but as a fortress against besieging enemies with guns and battering rams. Through a high gate with a barbican we passed into a wide court and through a maze of buildings came to the portal of the cathedral, against which drays were loading with bales and boxes.

We followed the sound of voices up to the great altar screen guarding the sanctuary forbidden to women. Such is the rule of the Orthodox Church, and such is the force of tradition long enforced that Woskova—though ten years a Communist agitator—in reflex obedience to old habits, hesitated to enter.

"Oh, come on in!" boomed out a big bluff voice. "That isn't a church. It's a museum."

Thus we came to meet the special Commission for Liquidation of the Monasteries. It was composed of six members—half of them Communists, all sons of local Suzdal peasants working under the direction of Romonovsky, archeologist and art expert.

"The best art treasures go to Moscow, or the new museum here," he explained, "the saleable material is sold for the school fund, the rest goes into the junk heap."

"This, for example, goes there," said the peasant Potashin, giving a battered archbishop's mitre a kick that sent it spinning through the altar-gates into the middle of the nave. Here was a curious agglomeration of nondescript ikons, amulets, tattered cowls and surplices, candle ends, moth-eaten altar cloths, Lives of Monks, chromos of Saint Seraphim conversing with a bear, another Saint braiding his ankle-long beard to keep it from dragging on the ground—the huge pile strewn with dead and dying pearls and emitting the acrid sickening odor of stale incense.

"Have a cigarette!" said a tall man in Red Army uniform. "I smoke them all day. Keeps the damned incense smell out of my nostrils. A whole year I've been on this job and I'm sick of it."

"But we've got to go slowly," put in Romonovsky, "or we'll make a mistake. Even so we almost lost this ikon here. Luckily we scratched it and saw it had been painted over. Some ignorant monk most likely. Scraping it carefully we uncovered a rare example of the Novgorod period. Worth its weight in gold."

"Here's one worth its weight in wood," laughed a square-bearded peasant from Palexo lugging out an enormous ikon of the Last Judgment, depicting the devil as a monkey with a spiked tail shoving heretics, thieves, Tartars and drunkards into the flames of hell. "My own father painted it. The monks gave him eight hundred rubles and with six workmen he finished it in a month. I remember it well: fifty rubles were laid out for vodka and they all went on a three days' drunk in the woods."

"What your fathers build up you are destroying," I put in provocatively.

"And with the greatest joy," burst forth the Red Armyist.

Such venom in the speaker, that I at once set him down as a former priest or Seminarist —in Russia generally a safe assumption. Particular virulence against religion is almost always the direct product of an ecclesiastical institution. Theological seminaries, it seems, were wholesale incubators of skeptics and atheists. To them the Communist Party is indebted for nearly all its leading anti-religious propagandists, now as zealous against the faith as one time for it.

Such was the case with this man Tikhomirov. Marked by extreme devoutness as a peasant boy, at seventeen years of age he was sent to the Florinsky Seminary in Vladimir. He liked religious art and specialized in it. Still more he liked the old Archbishop in his angry moments roaring at him in strange languages and in his softer moods playing chess.

One summer the young candidate for priest-hood was sent out to a little hermitage in the deep woods of Novgorod. Hither also in late June came the peasant girls to mow the grass in the forest clearings. They came with gala spirit. For the monks too were in the meadows, wetting the scythes of the girls, plaiting flowers in their hair, and on cold nights inviting them to sleep in the hermitage. Hay-making by day. Fun-making by night. An idyl of love and laughter. But always the danger of a sudden visit from the Archbishop. To guard against this sentinels were posted along the road. One dark night they fell asleep, and the Archbishop came down upon the place, taking it by storm. The monks rushed into the chapel, the girls squealing up into the bell-tower or scrambling over the walls, and after them the infuriated Archbishop with his staff laying out right and left.

The impression of moral vigor made by the old Archbishop was spoiled by the motive he gave for it. "The church is our blacksmith-shop in which we get our living. We have got to keep it in order."

This unhappy figure of speech was more of a shock to the sensitive young idealist than the escapades of the monks. War, the church blessing the slaughter of millions of *mujiks*, life in the wide world, had put the finishing touches on his doubts. There remained not a vestige of faith in religion. Apparently only a deep cynicism.

Now a deeper tinge to this cynicism by the exposures the Revolution had made in the monasteries—in this particular monastery, in the relics of the founder, the Blessed Saint Evfimy, beside the pried-up lid of whose shrine we were standing.

The full impact of this is clear only to one who understands the peculiar doctrine of the Russian Church about relics. It holds that the text, "Thou shalt not suffer thine holy one to see corruption," is not a figure of speech, but a fact. Holiness in life brings wholeness in death. The reward of righteousness is a body incorruptible that age shall not wither nor time decay. As it was so shall it be forever, free from rust and rot.

With some bodies this is actually what happened. They were naturally embalmed in the chalk or lime-soil in which they were buried. Shut away from moisture, they were long preserved intact, flesh uncontaminated and skin uncracked. Thus, dug up decades or maybe centuries later, their pristine purity and freshness was hailed as evidence of God's favor. Ringing bells proclaimed the miracle, and in

solemn processional the remains were carried
into the cathedral and laid away in a reliquary
all swaddled in silks and silver except for a
tiny portion of a hand or brow exposed for the
devout to kiss.

From far and wide the pilgrims came bringing offerings of gold and silver and copper.
So grew the monastery in wealth and prestige
inciting the envy of its rivals. They too
yearned for relics, fervently praying for them.
When no answer came to their prayers they
sometimes answered them themselves. They
fabricated relics.

How this was done the Revolution has dis-
closed. With doctors and cameras and crow-
bars, it came down upon the shrines and in
presence of officials of church and state the
tombs were opened. Wonders indeed brought
to light!

Instead of the uncorrupted bodies of the
Saints, moldering skeletons and bones sometimes not of men but animals! Sticks of wood
wound with cloth and cotton-wool and covered

with wax. Figures of corsets and skirts and ladies' stockings. With what Gargantuan laughter the jolly friars and their consorts must have made the Saints in effigy? With what gross frauds the credulity of the faithful were fed! On what crumbling foundations these temples raised, reared their cupolas and crosses to the sky! To what mercenary ends was exploited the name and fame won by the vigils and virtues and self-denial of the sturdy monks of old!

Such a one was Evfimy, founder of this monastery. A hair-shirted hermit, shriving his body for the good of his soul. A toil-lover, a well-digger, a stone-chiseler, baking bread for the hungry, tending the victims of the Black Death. A lover of peace reconciling princes and warriors and at eighty-eight years dying with the words: "God is love. Love is beauty. Love one another!"

That was in 1401. In 1507 the Archimandrite proclaimed to the world the finding of Evfimy's body fresh and uncorrupted as it had been buried a century ago. It was laid away in an imposing shrine that each decade grew more magnificent adding to itself new relics: his miter, his breviary, the great crosier which smote Cyprian the Glutton; the iron chains which mortified his flesh.

From all over the Russian land the pilgrims came to gaze upon the silver sarcophagus and the face of the Saint embossed in precious stones upon the cover. In gratitude they gave the monks their coins, and listened to the tales of marvels issuing from the shrine:

Gerasim the Idiot restored to his senses; Ivan the Paralytic set up on his legs again; Patric the Fisherman cured of palsy. In an apparition Evfimy had come revealing the hiding place of the stolen monastic treasure; in the flesh, rubbing his balsam into Nikodim's aching limbs; while the cures wrought by his healing honey-*kvas* were without number.

In detail all these miracles are recorded in Saint Evfimy's Five Hundredth Anniversary Book issued by the Ecclesiastical Censor of St.

Petersburg in 1904. It closes with these words:
"So ends the chronicles written by mortal hand.
But never in all the ages will end the wonders
that flow forth from this incorruptible body."

"Now I'll show you the incorruptible body,"
said Tikhomirov, turning to the shrine.
Throwing off silken winding-sheet, fumbling
through cotton-wool and wadding, he brought
to light a few brown, bleached bones and a
crumbling skull—a sorry exhibit even as a
skeleton.

"When I was a boy," continued Tikhomirov,
"my mother brought me to this shrine. She
told me that here was one so holy that God had
preserved him for five hundred years. A deep
impression it made on me, for my dog had just
died and in four days he smelt bad. With fear
and quaking I stood on tiptoe and kissed the
little round hole in this cloth and felt as though
I were kissing the very hand of God. And see!
all the time beneath this cloth this skull was
grinning at me."

Picking up a bone he brought it crashing

down upon the coffin. "Sacrilege!" exclaimed one of the Communists provocatively.

"Sacrilege!" reëchoed Tikhomirov. "It was the yarns and fables and greed of the dirty, bloated priests that did sacrilege to Evfimy. I do sacrilege to no honest man."

"Well, he was an honest man. Is he to blame for what the priests did to him after death? He deserves to have his bones left in peace."

"Those are no more Evfimy's bones than yours," retorted Tikhomirov. "The first bones the fakirs dug up in the cemetery. The first ones they laid their lying hands on. Maybe a dog's bones! They made a fool and dupe out of me."

"But why get mad about it? So long as you didn't know it was a hoax, you were happy. Much happier than you are now."

"You would make a better priest than a Communist," roared Tikhomirov. "It was all lies and corruption and deceit."

"But there were honest men in the church,"

I put in mildly. "They must have protested against its crimes and deceptions."

"Of course there were!" he answered. "But what became of them? Come with me and I'll show you what end they came to."

Down into a deep crypt he led us, stumbling and groping through the dark until stopped by a green molded wall. Lighting a candle, he thrust it through a grate opening into a black musty dungeon hung with rusting chains and ring bolts. A blast of cold foul air and the guttering candle went out.

"That's how the good men flickered out. And see the deviltry of it! They put the torture chamber exactly under the altar. Spiritual love of the brethren!"

The stone cage evidently was reserved for hardened heretics. For others, there were the usual iron barred cells—a long corridor of them. The massive walls built to keep Tartars from getting into the monasteries came more and more to serve another purpose—to keep reformers and protestants from getting out.

Hither, too, were brought rebels against the state, like the Decembrists, and other unfortunates who had incurred the royal displeasure, including many divorced wives of the Tsars. Unhappy Tsarinas! With their thrones losing their freedom. No Tsar, it seems, could rest easy until the high stone walls of a convent stood between him and his former consort. When of her own free will she would not betake herself to a nunnery, she was taken there by force.

Thus came to Suzdal, Ann, fifth wife of Ivan the Terrible; Avdotia, wife of Peter the Great . . . a long line of noble and royal spouses, ending their strange stormy careers in the quiet of the Suzdal cloisters. In the archives were lengthy chronicles reciting their lusts, loves, intrigues, sainthood, devilhood, sufferings and miracles. Piles of ancient scrolls and modern brochures, impossible to wade through. I drew one out at random—a record written by Abbess Melitini on "The Life of the Great Princess Solomona, known in the Veil as Sophie."

It begins with seven superlatives acclaiming the virtues of this orphan girl, a descendant of the Golden Horde. In the quiet seclusion of the *terem* she grew up a flower of grace, comeliness, modesty and piety. For such prizes the royal emissaries were hunting high and low over the Russian land. Great Prince Vassily was to take unto himself a bride, and of all the maidens good and beautiful, the loveliest and the best was to sit beside him on the throne.

By imperial *ukase*, Solomona, with fifteen hundred other maidens, was brought to the court in Moscow. A first general review reduced this number to five hundred. A second culling left a hundred and eight who were quartered in nine chambers of the Kremlin. Now the intensive inspection began in earnest. Solemn oaths from parents to conceal no defects in their daughters; attestations from physicians as to the virginity of the candidates; *boyars* debating their respective charms and merits; and Vassily, hidden behind secret panels and portières, making his own appraisal.

On the day of the great decision solemn services were held in the cathedral. Over black velvet carpets one by one the maidens came curtseying past the throne, waving their silken *mantikas*. "All eyes were fixed on the Great Prince, all hearts were frozen." Almost last came Solomona, and as she bowed low Vassily stepped down from the throne, lifted up the trembling girl, gave her his ring and a golden cross for all the court to kiss.

Thus at sixteen the orphan Tartar girl became queen of Moscow, the great *boyarinas* her ladies-in-waiting, the trumpeters heralding her comings and goings, the great prelates bringing her symbolic presents of bread, *kvas* and cabbage. A life of perfect bliss and harmony for the royal pair.

One rift however in the hymeneal lute that widened with the years. Solomona was childless. A-hunting in the woods Vassily would break into tears lamenting: "The birds have their young, the bears their cubs, the fishes swim with their little ones in the deeps. Only I am without issue!"

Imploring the saints for a child, Solomona went on long pilgrimages, lavishing alms on cripples and beggars, covering the shrines with her own handiwork in silk and satin. Still no heir to the throne and the *boyars* were mumbling: "Let the unfruitful vine be cast from the vineyard!"

Vassily long held out against divorce. But, dazzled by the charms of Elena (mother-to-be of Ivan the Terrible), he capitulated. Solomona was ordered to be shorn and hooded and taken to a nunnery, an insult that set her dormant Tartar blood a-boiling and turned her into a lashing, tearing tigress that the bishops could not tame with whips.

Once within the convent, time wore down her fury, and graciously as she carried the crown she wore the veil. In life a very gentle perfect nun and after death famed as the Suzdal Wonder Worker. Besides the usual miracles of healing at her shrine one glorious act of high revenge is recorded. That was in 1609 when Lisovsky was turning the Russian cities into ashes. Up surged the Tartar blood in Solomona's ghostly veins. Out of the tomb she rose, a hooded wraith and with burning candle fell upon the invader, scorching and flaying his right arm till it shriveled up and he fled in terror from the land.

With this story ends the record. An excellent chronicler, the Abbess Melitini, with a modern reporter's flair for news and a feminist delight in the gusty passions of Solomona.

Next morning we set forth to Pokrov nunnery—the shrine of Solomona. All the way Romonovsky was pointing out the technique of cupolas and domes, exulting over the treasures that lay beneath them. A devout votary of art, he judged others by their attitude towards it. All honor to the monks and nuns of old who devised these glories in stone and brick, in gold and lacquer. Deep contempt for their unworthy successors of to-day who painted over the ikons of the masters and marred the ancient architecture by hideous towers and bastions. Wreckers and wastrels despoiling the treasures they had inherited. With a sense of high service to the cause of art he was taking the control of them out of the hands of "these ignoramuses, the hooded vandals and barbarians of to-day."

This flow of imprecations was interrupted at the convent gate by a sudden "Good morning! Ivan Pokrovich!"

The greeting came from a tall comely person with big brown eyes peering out from under a snow-white hood, and a rope of big black beads dangling from her neck. The Abbess of the convent.

"Good morning, Marya Ivanovna," replied Romonovsky, "I'll take the keys to Trinity to-day."

"That was the pride of our nunnery," sighed the Abbess, "the heart of it all."

"And a rare example of sixteenth century

style," Romonovsky briskly went on. "Notice particularly the griffons and spandrels above the door. Also the cubic columns . . ."

"Through that door," interrupted the Abbess, "I must have passed a thousand times to midnight mass."

". . . the cubic columns," continued Romonovsky, "which harmonize with the balustrades of the stairway."

". . . and up that stairway," persisted the Abbess, "for fourteen years I went every evening to vespers."

". . . all in Byzantine style," continued Romonovsky, "but showing already definite Russian influence."

Thus the conversation, or rather the two monologues, jumped along on two distinct planes never remotely impinging on one another. Grotesque, impossible! It was a choice between the archeologist and the Abbess.

Art and architecture, I reasoned, would be here to gaze upon for centuries to come. But not the Abbess. Presently she would disappear and with her the last of the long line that reached back into the thirteenth century. So I chose the Abbess and through a labyrinth she led us to a house banked high with lilacs.

"The priory!" she exclaimed stately and imperiously. "Here I received His Highness the Emperor."

We entered the house swarming now with orphans of the war, waifs of the hunger time, living on black bread and soup. Amazing the amount of noise, laughter and piano-thumping that came out of this meager diet.

"Once it was so quiet and orderly," sighed the Abbess. "And now look at it! Disorder and dirt and shouting."

"And once," blurted out the Communist girl irrepressibly, "it sheltered five or six nuns, and now it shelters a hundred children. Isn't that much better?"

"This is the service of man," replied the Abbess with quiet dignity. "But there is something higher. There is the service of God."

"And what's that?" queried the Communist.

"Why, that was what all our whole life was devoted to. Up in the morning at four. Matins from five to eight. Selling ikons and candles and holy water to pilgrims. Vespers. Then our needle-work. Almost any price we asked for our lace and embroideries. Fourteen years with hardly a moment of grief or worry. Now see what I've come to!"

Through the wooden dormitories she led us to her little "cell" fragrant with flowers and spotlessly clean as the white bands on her nun's attire. She served us carrot tea and bread prepared with sugar-beat juice, sweet as cake. Then she laid out before us her little treasures and heirlooms, crosses of crystal, bone and Ural stone. Last and most precious of all a china cup.

"The very one the Tsar drank out of when he visited us in 1913? Such a kind and good and gentle soul. But, oh, so tired. He stayed with us a long time, resting."

The Abbess was transfigured as she spoke, a luminous tenderness in her big brown eyes, her whole person vibrant with a strange magnetism of blended sensualism and mysticism, piety and voluptuous feeling. Small wonder the tired Tsar long tarried in her room.

Brooding over sweet remembrances she fell into a reverie out of which she was jarred by the query of the Communist.

"But the Revolution! What did you do when the Tsar was overthrown?"

"We prayed to God."

"And then the second revolution—the Bolshevik?"

"We didn't know one from the other. We only knew that Antichrist was loose, that terrible things were going on in the world, and we prayed God that our nunnery should be spared."

"That was terribly egoistic, wasn't it?" continued the Communist relentlessly. "All the world filled with hungry and wounded and dying and you off in your little corner praying God to look after you."

"Maybe it was.   But that's the way we were taught—to pray."

"Well, it didn't help you very much, did it?" said the Communist brutally.

"That was God's will," replied the Abbess softly.   Then for the first time losing self-control she turned upon her heckler and burst out:

"But you!   You don't know the meaning of that!"

"Quite so, but I know the meaning of economic determinism, class solidarity and the proletarian revolution!"

Strange meaningless phrases that baffled the Abbess and left her staring blankly at the Communist as a creature from another world.   One thing only the two women had in common. Both were daughters of peasants.   That was all.   The one at fourteen years of age had gone into a factory, the other into a nunnery.   The one had made her own way through twenty countries; the other had lived in a little world bounded by high stone walls.   The one had known hunger, strikes, jail and carried the scars of them; the other had known the sheltered life in a privileged order. The dreams of the one had been filled with pictures of the blessed life together with the saints in glory; the visions of the other concerned the building in this world of a brotherhood for all.

In the persons of these two women the thirteenth century came face to face with the twentieth. Wider than the gulf between the Abbess and the archeologist was this that stretched between her and the agitator. They were universes apart, speaking alien tongues, thinking alien thoughts. A tense impossible situation, happily resolved by the Communist rising and walking out of the "cell."

One more ordeal of the Abbess was over, and in glad relief she flung off all caution or reserve. A long litany of her woes mingled with weird stories of punishments visited upon the persecutors of God's people: The blasphemer struck blind by the ikon of the Virgin that wept tears of blood; the son miraculously born to Saint -

Sophie to avenge her wrongs; the comet with a tail like a cross that terrorized the Tartar raiders into panic and death; the sacred seagulls of Solovetz that saved the monastery from the bombardment of the British Squadron —they flew out by thousands, completely hiding the island with their wings, or pecking at the eyes of the gunners to put them off their aim.

I listened attentively, not crossing or contradicting her as did those Antichrists, the archeologist and the agitator, while the Abbess continued to pour forth her most secret hopes and hates and pent-up passions:

"God is trying his people. But the Mother of God will not forget us. Faithful unto Her, she will be faithful unto us. All the pains we suffer shall be inflicted on our enemies a hundredfold. A miracle will come, a sheet of lightning, an earthquake to destroy the Antichrists, and restore us the nunnery. But how long! How long! Surely the time must be at hand!"

The Abbess paused and gathered up her little heirlooms. Last of all she wiped the china cup and set it in its place upon the ikon shelf, remarking, half musingly, half in query:

"How long will it be before he returns to us?"

For the moment I was puzzled, not guessing that she was speaking of the Tsar. Then I said:

"But he's dead!"

"No, he isn't dead," she asserted firmly. "He was saved by a soldier. Anya heard all about it when she was in Moscow. I'll call her in."

There entered a bent, wrinkled old nun who, after drinking some cold carrot tea, related the legend that afterwards I was to hear in varying versions. This is the substance of it:

When Kerensky was in power he placed the Tsar in a little cottage in a side street of Tsarskoe Selo. There in a tiny garden with shrubs and flower-beds and vegetables the Tsar would work all day with spade and water-sprinkler. One day as he approached the gate, the sentinel, lowering his bayonet, challenged:

"Citizen! Stand back!"

"Citizen!" exclaimed the Tsar, with a bitter smile. "Since when am I 'citizen'?"

The soldier was deeply touched. He, a simple soldier addressing his monarch as "citizen." Red with shame he bowed before the Tsar, saying:

"Forgive me, Your Majesty! If you want to be free give me your overcoat and sprinkler and take my uniform and rifle!"

Hastily donning the disguise, the Tsar said, "When I am on the throne again I'll make you Minister and give you a palace!"

The soldier began watering the flowers, while the Tsar stood on guard. When the relief patrol came up he walked out of the gate and went abroad. But later he returned to Russia, to the Monastery of Sarov. There in cassock and wooden sandals, feeding on bread and water, he prays for sinful Russia, waiting till God shall make him Emperor again.

Also a new story about two billions of gold, deposited in a Paris bank by Maria Fedorovna, the Tsar's mother, as a bequest to the Russian people on one condition: they should put an end to the Soviet.

"It would be just like her," nodded the Abbess. "The Tsar himself was always giving things away. He gave me a beautiful golden cross for the altar."

Thus amidst the wreck of their little world, the Abbess and her sisterhood now reached back to sweet memories of the happy past, now buoyed up their spirits with apocalyptic visions of the happy future, restoring the Tsar to his throne, the nuns to their nunneries, in dreams and legends saving themselves from utter desolation and despair. It needed but one reason for hope, one touch of reality to drive out all these phantasies.

This hope and reality entered the room in the person of a hard-headed, hard-legged nun who had footed it most of the way from Nijni. Astounding news she brought with her. The

Pechersky Convent was now the Pechersky Commune! And the nuns were Communards! The old order had been reconstituted as an artel of workers. Under the new name they retained their "cells" and one of their chapels. They had been granted a tract of land. They were tilling it and they were contented.

If this could be done in Nijni, why not in Suzdal? On the way she had put this question to the Volost Soviet and the answer had been: "Nothing in the law to prevent it." As a commune they had rights to a certain norm of plowland and pasture—maybe garden plots in which to grow mint and chicory.

A sudden full face about in the conversation. Out of the clouds the little sisterhood came down to earth. Literally so. The room hummed with questions about land. How much land and where? How divide the time between chapel services and field work? Where to find money for plows and seeds?

"We can find it in our needles," said the nun from Nijni. "We can sew Soviet emblems and slogans on red banners like the Pechersky Convent is doing."

Some murmurings against this.

"Why not?" insisted the nun from Nijni. "If we are going to use hammers and sickles in our work, why not embroider them on banners?"

A chorus of "Yeses!" For the first time a little laughter. There were even good words for Communists. And they had just been calling them Antichrists, calling on God to destroy them! Such was the revolution wrought by the prospect of land and income. Most marked the ravages of economic determinism on the Abbess. Three hours earlier rigidly limiting "services of God" to vigils, prayers, fasting and candle-burning. Now to these works of merit adding—plowing, harvesting, threshing.

A return to the soil. At the same time a return to the thirteenth century, to the first principles of the monastic orders, to the traditions of the forest-felling, stone-cutting, swamp-draining monks of old. For those first convents and hermitages were built by the straining muscles of the inmates who lived within them. In the sweat of their faces the Black Sea Coast was planted with orange and mandarin groves. With their calloused hands the rocky barren islands of Solovetz were reclaimed from the Arctic Seas. With peasant respect for physical toil went respect for the toilers. Even Peter the Great had to be cautious in his mild measures against the monasteries, fearing to rouse the people to resistance.

Centuries pass. Riches come rolling into the monasteries, fat rolling up on the friars. The old story of wealth, corruption and moral decline. And everywhere crying opportunities for a toiling, serving, teaching order. Around Suzdal an illiterate peasantry, sixty per cent unable to read or write, a primitive system of agriculture, roads through which the horses flounder belly-deep in mud.

But what matters this to the fable-spinning, flesh-wallowing, ease-loving monks of to-day? Even the suggestion that it was their concern

would be met with amazement or lofty disdain.
So complete their break with the toiling tradition, so total their estrangement from the
masses.

Now the Revolution had a terrible need of
these masses. All the bells of the monasteries
beating a furious alarm, calling the peasants
to rise and come to their aid against the Reds.
But not a hand raised in their defense. All
loyalty and allegiance has long since been for-
feited. Without hindrance the Soviet proceeds—not as Peter the Great to restrict the
monastic orders—but to abolish, suppress, ex-
tinguish them altogether.

I enter the market-square just as the drays
laden with the spoils from Evfimy Monastery
go driving through the peasant throng. On the
rough cobbles they swing from side to side like
huge censers, throwing off the fumes of incense
from bales of cassocks, robes and altar-cloths.
In vain I scan the faces of the peasants for some
sign of dissent or disapproval. They sniff the
pungent odor. They joke and chaffer. They

pass the rusty alms' box bearing the legend, "Give to the Glory of Martyr of God Evfimy," and gather round a red and black poster showing a hand thrust out through prison bars appealing, "Give for the relief of revolutionists in foreign jails."

That night we walked on top of the earth embankment winding round the town. Against these ramparts rolled the Golden Hordes of Batai Khan, their slopes now gay with daisies and dandelions growing out of soil soaked with the blood of Christian and infidel. In full splendor the June moon rose behind the low hills and striking cupola and turret, flung strange cubic spheric shadows across our path. The river like a silver snake sprawled across the plain. On the far meadows, blurred outlines of the grazing herds. A perfume-laden breeze blowing from the honeysuckle bastion. The chiming of a bell singularly soft and sweet. And yellow gleaming amidst the jumble of buildings below us, the little candle-lit window of the Abbess.

To Tikhomirov I spoke about the plans of the Abbess and her toiling commune.

He shrugged his shoulders. "Too late! New times! The bricks that went into monasteries we will put into roads and bridges and electric stations. The gold and pictures they put on the altar-screen we will put into schools and clubs. In Russia the convent, cloister days are gone forever."

"But the age-old needs of the soul! Since time began, man has built retreats and refuges to flee from the sins and sorrows and torments of the world."

"If it were a world without sorrow and torment, a just and happy world, he wouldn't want to flee from it. That's the kind of world we are going to build."

"Going to—yes. But what have you built?"

"Not much as yet. We've been busy clearing away the débris. Besides, we've had but ten years while they had ten centuries. Give us twenty, thirty years more and we'll build a world of peace between nations and races, a classless, warless world, a world without slaves or idlers . . ."

He took off his red-starred helmet. His mask of cynicism dropped away. In glowing words rose up a vision of the future—fair and alluring as the golden city a few days ago gleaming before us on the distant plains—the vision of the good society that through centuries has haunted the dreamers and lovers of mankind.

The Monastic Age may have passed in Russia, but not the Age of Faith.